GASTON LACHAISE

GASTON LACHAISE

THE MAN AND HIS WORK

GERALD NORDLAND

George Braziller / New York

for Ann

Frontispiece: Gaston Lachaise, 1927. Photo, Paul Strand.

Copyright © 1974 by Gerald Nordland

Published simultaneously in Canada by Doubleday Canada, Limited

For information address the publisher:
George Braziller, Inc., One Park Avenue, New York 10016

Library of Congress Catalog Card Number: 74–80661

Standard Book Number: 0–8076–0761–4, cloth
                                0–8076–0762–2, paper

Printed in the U.S.A.

First Printing

DESIGNED BY RONALD FARBER

This book was produced in conjunction with the exhibition GASTON
LACHAISE, held at the Herbert F. Johnson Museum of Art, Cornell
University; the Frederick S. Wight Galleries, University of California
at Los Angeles; the Museum of Contemporary Art, Chicago; and the
Walker Art Center, Minneapolis, and made possible by a grant from
the National Endowment for the Arts, a federal agency.

Contents

Preface

Our understanding of Lachaise has been severely limited by a number of interrelated factors: his early and untimely death; the unfashionable character of his explorations; the impressionistic nature of criticism of his work, save only the long unavailable Lincoln Kirstein monograph for the Museum of Modern Art; and the absence of an important exposure of his sculpture in a manner which permitted easy access and encouraged study.

Madame Isabel Lachaise, the artist's widow, conserved the content of the studio-workshop as best she could. She served the artist's reputation in every way possible to her. Were it not for her faith and effort it would hardly be possible to piece together the story of his life and the evolution of his art. With the sound advice of Lincoln Kirstein, Mme. Lachaise deposited her correspondence, scrapbooks, and memorabilia in the Library of American Letters, Yale University. She tenaciously held the whole body of Lachaise plasters together under her control.

It is a pleasure to acknowledge the important encouragement of Mr. Kirstein, who maintained a correspondence with me for several years in the late forties, when I was trying to decide what part I could play in the telling of Lachaise' story. Mr. Kirstein took some effort in guiding me, prepared the way for me at Yale with his friend, Donald Gallup, and introduced me to Mme. Lachaise with the weight of his own approval. My many meetings with Mme. Lachaise, in Lexington and in Georgetown, were touching experiences as well as immensely helpful to my gathering of information.

Among the family, friends, and colleagues of Gaston and Isabel Lachaise, I interviewed and corresponded with many and I want to thank the following for their unsparing gifts of time, research on my behalf into old diaries and letters, and their frequent hospitality: Stefan Bourgeois, E. E. Cummings, A. E. Gallatin, Phillip Goodwin, Joe Gould, Lincoln Kirstein, Allys Lachaise, Henry McBride, Dorothy (Miller) Cahill, Marianne Moore, George L. K. Morris, Reuben Nakian, Marie Pierce, Gilbert Seldes, Paul Strand, Carl Van Vechten, Edward M. M. Warburg, Mr. and Mrs. Oliver Wellington, M. R. Werner, and Marguerite and William Zorach.

Special thanks go to Mr. Donald Gallup, Curator of the Library of American Letters, now housed in the Beinecke Rare Book Library, Yale University, for his patience, good advice, and a welcome typewriter. Thanks are also due to Mr. John B. Pierce, Jr., Managing Trustee of the Lachaise Foundation, for his unswerving devotion to the memory of Lachaise, the project of this book, and his continuing help in reading and correcting the text. I want to thank the Lachaise Foundation for the grant which I enjoyed during 1972 and 1973. Finally I must mention the assistance of Basil Petrov of M. Knoedler and Co., Inc., the friendly help of Mr. E. Weyhe, and the cooperation of Mr. Robert Schoelkopf, the Foundation's representative. I want also to express my gratitude to Mitzi Landau, Curator, Lachaise Foundation, for her assistance with photographs and permissions.

G. N.

I.

THE MAN and HIS LIFE

"All my life I shall be getting away from the academy," **Paris**
Gaston Lachaise confessed to Isabel, his future wife, as she
prepared in 1904 to return to her Boston home. His love for
her and joy in her presence led this Frenchman to renounce
Paris, abandon his "dream of Rome," and turn away from
the academic success for which he had prepared himself, in
order to follow Isabel to the United States in search of a new
life and, in turn, to produce a new sculptural vision. Outside of the academy, Lachaise was to establish one of the
memorable visions of Woman in all sculpture—a spiritual
elevation and exaltation of the physical being of womankind.

A simple man, Lachaise came to recognize that he had a
great mission. The peculiar combination of his talent and
his training, his physical stamina, courage, and his passionate adoration of Isabel led him to recognize a fearful
muse. He reexamined classical models through his academic
skills and his romantic intuitions. He was a totally devoted,
chivalrous, and idealistic young man, moved to transport by
physical love of a beautiful and intellectual older woman
who inspired him to create a monument in her image. His
work is a lyric of developing force, which praises woman
and exalts her goddess-like procreative energies.

Lachaise' Woman presents an alternative to Greco-Roman
geometry through a marriage to the sensuous style of Indian
temple sculpture. Lachaise embraces all cultures and all experiences, East and West, Christian and Pagan. He perceived
a mystic unity of meaning and necessity and for him love

and knowledge became a single thing in his art. As Marsden Hartley wrote of him, "He saw the entire universe in the form of woman." From the very first, Lachaise' Woman had the energy and impact of a religious icon, the power to infuriate as well as the capacity to elicit sacred feelings.

Gaston's father, Jean, was a prominent French wood-carver and cabinetmaker who designed the Eiffel apartment in the famed Paris tower. Jean was himself one of three sons of Jean Michel Lachaise and Antoinette Danglais. Originally from the mountainous Auvergne territory, the couple had moved to Paris in the early 1850s. In the war of 1870 their son, Jean, served in the French army. After demobilization he returned to Paris and established a furniture workshop in the Faubourg St. Antoine. Within a year he married Marie Barre, the Paris-born daughter of Louis Barre and Celestine Engel. Jean and Marie had four children. The first two were boys who died in infancy. The third child, Allys, was born in 1881, and Gaston, their fourth child, was born in Paris on March 19, 1882.

Despite his talent and dedication to his craft, Jean Lachaise, due to the vagaries of the French economy, had to struggle to find a dependable business arrangement through which to support his family; he moved his workshop and his family from the city to the suburbs, back to the city, and finally to the suburbs again, in search of a successful formula.

Jean's dedication to his work and his mastery of wood-working and cabinetry came to serve as a model of the masculine role and commitment for Gaston. Using his hands in making works of virtue became an archetypal conduct in the young man's mind. Jean had dreamed of following fine art as a career and his dream was passed on to his son.

Gaston's sister, Allys, told the story of her young brother disappearing from their parents' house in the suburb of St. Mande when he was five years old. Suddenly missing the boy's humming, his mother went searching only to find him, finally, in his father's woodworking studio at the rear of the garden. Gaston had never strayed there before. He was cutting away with one of his father's heavy chisels at a piece of wood. Marie was fearful that Gaston would injure himself and moved to take the tool from the child. The boy's father, standing quietly by the door, stopped her, saying, "No, let him do it; I am watching." Little Gaston was making a *bénitier*, a font for holy water, to be placed at the foot of an effigy of the Christ child. Jean Lachaise was moved when he saw what the boy could do. Gaston later gave the shell-like font, his first work, to a girl his own age. The little girl treasured and retained it, even after she became a nun in Burgundy, according to Lachaise' sister.

In subsequent years Gaston accompanied and assisted his father, learning by example the patience craftsmanship requires. Eventually Jean's distinction in woodcarving brought him the commissions to decorate the apartment of the Chancellor of Spain[1] and to design and panel the interior of the Eiffel apartment in the tower then being built in Paris. The climb to the apartment was a fearful one for Gaston, for he was terrified by heights. His fear was overcome in his awe for his father's task and for the role Jean played in this dramatic enterprise.

Overcoming his own feelings of fear and apprehension in order to carry out his work, fulfill his commissions, and achieve his goals became a pattern in the life of Gaston Lachaise. His father's dream for him and Gaston's own dimly perceived goals found fulfillment: he became one of the most original and provocative sculptors of the new century. However, fate did not permit his father to witness the realization of their dreams; Jean Lachaise died prematurely at the age of fifty-six.

Gaston and Allys were close in years and spirit while young, and they played together until Allys first went to school. Their attachment for one another remained strong through life though their aesthetic and professional interests diverged. Allys was inclined toward music. She and their mother Marie followed Gaston to America and she taught both music and the French language.[2] She remained a spinster and never knew nor really comprehended a passionate lifetime love. Allys cared for her mother, worked in elite girls' schools, and sustained a modest life as a virtuous woman of the French provincial type so clearly and touchingly portrayed by Flaubert's Felicité in *Un Coeur Simple*.

Lachaise' memories of childhood days spent without Allys after she went to school were full of images such as ". . . delight and fear at venturing . . . among the weeds (after entering a vacant lot through a broken fence) in search of lovely flowers." Writing many years later, he described a similar event: ". . . getting lost one evening among the mob at a country fair; dreadful fear to be taken by the Gypsy . . . next morning tenderly recomforted by mother teaching to me gently my name and address, this I learned quickly while standing up between her laps. . . ."[3] The words were handwritten on Brevoort Hotel stationery in the late years of his life—his awkwardness with English was never overcome, yet the innocent force of that childhood experience is rendered with touching appeal.

In other passages of his "autobiography" Lachaise recalled his earliest memory of public school, being given blank paper and instructions he could not somehow fathom, experiencing feelings of frustration and then the helpless weeping that followed. A few years later, in another public school in Paris, he recalled becoming ". . . very unruled . . . gambling wildly with marbles." It was then that he ventured through another (perhaps forbidden) fence ". . . to collect seedlings—little trees to be planted and cherished in a flower box by the window at home." [4]

Lachaise' early childhood experiences provided him with an important example in his father's prestige as a skillful technician and woodworker and encouraged Lachaise' interest in tools. The boy's devotion to flowers and trees, his early indifference to books and study, combined with his adventurousness and his intuitive spirit to help him develop a sense of self-directed craftsmanship. He was sensitive to nature and to art but he was more a man of action than an intellectual.

Writing in the early 1930s and without subsequent editing, Lachaise recounted that he had been ". . . taken by my parents to the *Cirque d'hiver*. Saw Buffalo Bill: somptous galloping around on a beautiful white horse and shooting down, eggs shells tosed up in the air by a cavalcading Indian. These were trills to a little boy five years old—the profusion of light of music—the smell of parfum mingled with the ammonia of the stables—and also trilling—the wonderful round bossomed and round heaped lady—tossing herself up and down from a beautifully decorated big horse galloping gently in circles. . . ." [5] This intensely remembered experience of "a boy five years old" and written for himself, only a few years before his death, must have had powerful meaning for the life and work of the man. Experienced in 1887, Lachaise' visit to the *Cirque d'hiver* was relived in 1918 in the 10½ inch tall sculpture *Equestrienne* (Fig. 64) and remembered with such intensity that both the "parfum" of the event and the ammonia of the stables could still mingle in his recollections near the close of his life.

Lachaise recalled, "Father taking a position in a small town—some miles from Paris made the family move . . . the remain of an ancien early Rennaissance castle—tranquil big rooms and the delight of real country life right out the door —very happy days these were—my behavior at school very good. The school master was a sort of giant, very debonnaire and warm hearted. The small town (Crepy-en-Valois) was sleeping gently between two old Gothique church at each end" of the main street.

"When I became to be 13 years old—the problem of what I was to be as a man was taken up very seriously. I wanted to be a naval officer in the French Navy—but was persuaded that mathematique would be in my way—Then I wanted to be an inventor—dreaded mathematique came up again. My father advised me to follow is trade; a wood carver, and dreaming that maybe, he could lead me to sculpture statuary 'Art' which have been out of reach for him." [6]

"Accordingly I beguin to travel each day to Paris to the school of 'Art applique a l'industry—Bernard Palissy.'" Lachaise studied with the Director of the Ecole Bernard Palissy, Jean Paul Aube, an academic sculptor, and with Alphonse Moncel, the master in sculpture. The latter teacher became a friend of the Lachaise family and advised and assisted both Gaston and his sister in later years. The Ecole Bernard Palissy was "one of the most thorough and imaginative training grounds for the artist-craftsman in the whole of Europe. A remarkable standard of practical work in carving stone, wood and ivory, in drawing, painting, anatomy and the history of art was maintained by an excellent academic faculty." [7]

Aube permitted Lachaise, while he was a student at the Ecole, to collaborate on a statuette titled *Les Reconnaissances* which was later purchased by the Budapest Museum. The Director of the Ecole Bernard Palissy ordered the plate for the statuette to be engraved: "Les Reconnaissances by Aube in collaboration with G. Lachaise." [8] Lachaise' master, Moncel, used Lachaise as the model for his figural monument to the poet Alfred de Musset, and Moncel corresponded with Lachaise for more than ten years following the latter's departure from the school. Moncel continued to respond to letters from Mlle. Allys Lachaise long after Lachaise moved to the United States.

The course of study at the Bernard Palissy was structured on a four-year pattern. Lachaise applied for admission to the Académie Nationale des Beaux-Arts at the close of his third year at the Ecole with the cooperation of its director and of the master in sculpture. Lachaise was admitted to the Beaux-Arts in April 1898, at the age of sixteen, the same age at which Jean Antoine Houdon (1741–1828) was accepted by the Académie. Shortly after his acceptance at the Beaux-Arts Lachaise was permitted to become a pupil of Gabriel Jules Thomas, ". . . the most conservative of the classicists and head of one of the three sculpture ateliers" [9] in the Beaux-Arts. Alphonse Moncel had studied with Thomas, and doubtless this encouraged both Lachaise and Thomas despite Lachaise' remarkable youth. Two eminent sculptors on the faculty at the time were Louis-Ernest Barrias and Jean-Alexandre-Joseph Falguière. During the period of Lachaise' study at the Beaux-Arts, ". . . of the three hundred odd students of the time only Despiau, Landowski, and Lachaise have, in any real sense, become eminent." [10]

"Of all my schooling I am most endetted to Bernard Palissy, and reverend (sic) for the pratical element and the technical teaching which was given to me so profusely. After three years of these benefactions I could not realize yet wat I had been given to; as a base—I wanted to move quickly to the Beaux-Arts—This would be supreme and the dream of 'Rome' at the end of the rainbow." [11] Apparently the young sculptor felt that he learned more profound and influential truths in his study at the Ecole than he did at the Beaux-Arts and thus his mention of his indebtedness. However, the status of a student at the Académie Nationale was a matter of pride to Lachaise and to his family and it gave him the security and discretion to direct his own time in work at the Académie, in his own small studio on the Avenue du Maine, or in visits to the museums of Paris. Lachaise was judged a good student. He dressed the part of a Beaux-Arts student with long hair, wide velvet trousers, a voluminous black necktie, cape, sombrero, and cane.[12]

Four times during his enrollment at the Beaux-Arts Lachaise exhibited in the Paris Salon des Artistes Français. The first occasion was in 1897 when his *Portrait of Allys Lachaise* (Fig. 23) was shown on the recommendation of Gabriel Jules Thomas and Alphonse Moncel despite Salon rules which prohibited works of students so young. Within two years he could claim: "I placed myself 19 of the 20 selected for the competition of the much coveted French Prix de Rome. I was then 18 and moving among men up to 30." [13] In 1901, 1902 and 1904, Lachaise had works exhibited in the Salon des Artistes Français at the Grand Palais, and he repeatedly found a place on the lists of the first twenty among 300 candidates for the Prix de Rome.[14]

It was during this period that Lachaise had his first opportunity to examine the work of the past in the French museums. "For a time I remained in France lazily contemplating masterpieces of the past," he recalled later. "I became unruled again. I could not stand the Grec subject any longer—and the academie requirement of the weekly nude study. I drifted to studio parties, yet not to wildly— To Montmartre . . . Le Moulin Rouge—on few occasions and for better times to The Concerts Rouges . . . Verlaine, Baudelaire, Rimbaud became my ferveur." [15] This was then a romantic time of self search by Lachaise for a place in adult society. He explored the city's museums and galleries, read poetry and philosophy, participated in the student art life. One may presume that his lifelong devotion to the circus, the zoo, the burlesque, and to parks and gardens was formed in part during these years of academic achievement and intuitive search.

Three events of great importance occurred within the years 1901–04, and they combined to influence the artist's life. The first was the death of Lachaise' father, Jean, who contracted meningitis and died within a short time in the summer of 1901. His death was both a personal and a financial setback for the family and made it necessary that they relocate in a more modest apartment. Gaston was able to retain his studio.

The second and most crucial event occurred somewhere between 1900 and 1903: Lachaise met a Canadian-American woman named Isabel Dutaud Nagle. It is perhaps the greatest and most beautiful mystery of human experience when, in a world of strangers, two people meet, their souls touch, and suddenly they are no longer alone. The transformation of the universe, the brightness, clarity, and poignancy experienced can be extraordinary. Gaston Lachaise was to undergo such a baptism and to sustain his ardor until his death. His vision never dimmed; he was never to know the pain of returning to the state of being alone. Inspired by Isabel he would live to achieve a miracle in his work: he sculptured his vision of his beloved. He was able to create numbers of works which were depictions of her as she seemed to him: a twentieth-century Venus, in sculptures which are among the greatest tributes to woman created by man.

The date and location of their first meeting is uncertain. Mrs. Nagle remembered it as being in the Luxembourg Gardens in 1900, when she was twenty-eight and Lachaise eighteen. [16] Marsden Hartley, writing from conversations with her, claimed that the meeting was ". . . before some object at the Musée de Cluny (Paris)." [17] Mrs. Nagle, who later became Mme. Lachaise, recalled that Gaston at the time of their meeting was wearing an armband of crepe in mourning for his father. That could place their first meeting after September of 1901 and suggests that she who would become his primary inspiration came to Gaston at the moment when his first inspiration, his father, was taken from him.

Lachaise wrote in the 1930s "One Spring day . . . as I was coming out through the beautifull formal garden and the beautifull gate of the School, I passed a majestic woman that was walking slowly by the bank of the Seine. I succeeded to meet the majestic woman later—through her the splendor of life was uncovered for me and the road of wonder beguin widening and far out reaching. . . ." [18]

In 1928 Lachaise published another account: ". . . At twenty, in Paris, I met a young American person who immediately became the primary inspiration which awakened my vision and the leading influence that has directed my forces. Throughout my career, as an artist, I refer to this person by the word 'Woman'." [19] It could then have been in 1901 or perhaps in the spring of 1902—the year that Lachaise turned twenty—that he met his Isabel. In later years Isabel recalled that "He was a perfect Frenchman, yet I hated Frenchmen. He was so sober, nothing was ever said to hear himself say it. It was *honest!* He was very handsome. He had absolutely no color—very dark brown eyes, thick black hair, a firm mouth. He wore black much of the time, increasing the paleness of his complexion. He didn't like some of his photos from around 1900 because he said they were 'so frenchy'!"

Within a few weeks of their first meeting Lachaise asked permission to do a portrait head of Isabel which was executed in a sculpture measuring just six inches. In the succeeding two years Mrs. Nagle reported having seen Lachaise every day, visiting his studio, attending museums, musical programs, and dining together. The two lovers had few Parisian friends, except the sculptor of animals, Pierre Cristophe, with whom Lachaise shared a studio.

Isabel Dutaud Nagle was a Boston matron with a child and an older businessman husband. Raised as a Catholic, she had married at twenty but had never been happy in her marriage. Her sense of duty, of self, and of family and Church, combined with her belief that her husband would never permit her to take her son Edward with her, forced Isabel to delay her divorce until her son (born in 1893) was attending Harvard College. Edward, himself very intelligent, idolized Gaston Lachaise and his work, introduced it to his classmates and wrote an ambitious essay about Lachaise and his French tradition.[20] However, Edward's own adult life was tragic: he suffered a number of mental breakdowns in the late 1920s and early 1930s, was institutionalized, and never recovered.

Isabel Dutaud Nagle was not a large woman. She was a full-bosomed lady with generous proportions but not weighty. Remembering her in the 1950s one commentator said, "I remember Mme. L. as a giantess—a tremendous woman, and probably the most handsome one ever." [21] In fact she was a small woman weighing only 110 pounds and measuring hardly more than five foot two or three inches at the time Lachaise first met her. The fine nose, firm chin, even measurement of the eye, are apparently more memorable than height. She carried herself proudly, head high, chin slightly raised, exuding a sense of poised self esteem, she moved lightly on small feet and gave a sense of sailing into life on her own terms. Her hair was worn quite full on the head, with a roll at the base of the skull and her ears revealed. Nude photographs of Isabel from the first decade of the century show a diminutive version of the standing woman, *Elevation* (Fig. 17): slender legs, ample hips, well-muscled abdomen, arched back, full bust, shoulders held back and a proudly turned head in profile. Photographed against a paisley print, wearing what appears to be a near-Eastern headdress with decorative beads, her pose is regal and her sense of poise unquestionable.[22]

Isabel was a strong woman, a person of firm and certain character. She became ever more *Elevation*-like in later life, as though she had the example of Lachaise' sculpture to which she must conform. Her mind and person were holy to Lachaise and he translated her into his bronze goddess, lingering over every detail of anatomy with utmost concern and reverence for the sense of admiration, respect and devotion and unexampled good fortune that she brought into his heart and life.

Coming as he did from a traditional conservative French family, with perhaps a touch of prudery attached, Lachaise found Isabel, in her worldliness, her direct and passionate response to his admiration and desire for her, to be a companion beyond any comparison. Once they found each other there was no force that could separate them. "We shared *everything*. Every bit of music. We pleased ourselves as well as each other, physically, emotionally, intellectually. Nei-

ther of us had had a companion in (our) search for values
and love." "He had a reverence for women that was very
wonderful." "He gave me a wonderful security despite the
hardship. . . ." "He opened up another world (for me) and
he said the same of me, too." [23]

Gaston Lachaise, determined to wait for Isabel as long as
necessary, continued his studies, exhibited in the Salon, com-
peted in the Rome Awards. It seemed evident from his unusual successes that he was destined for the Prix de Rome—
"the dream at the end of the rainbow."

However, the third event of the early 1900s occurred. In
Lachaise' words: ". . . Shortly after this meeting (with Isabel) I was called to serve in the French Army—This, I felt
was very desastrous, and I set myself to become free as
quickly as possible. . . ." [24] Military service was then universal in France and Lachaise became eligible in 1903 on
his twenty-first birthday. As the only male in the family and
as a student in good standing he qualified for partial ex-
emption. Lachaise chafed under even the reduced requirement and expressed his distress at the lack of freedom and
the regimentation with which he suffered. The length of his
military service is uncertain but it was apparently less than
a twelve-month period. His *Certificat de Bonne Conduite*
from the 101ᵉ Regiment d'Infantry is dated September
1904.[25] It is likely that he served considerably less than the
time indicated by the Certificat, inasmuch as he wrote: "After few months of doing technical drawing for an army
physician I was rewarded by a leave of absence for the rest
of my military service and granted a scholarship from the
City of Paris. Life again was beautifull and more significant until my majestic friend returned to America; her
home." [26]

Lachaise had his new scholarship and every reason to expect that Rome was in his future through his work at the
Beaux-Arts. Nevertheless he elected to discontinue his studies
and to seek employment in order to earn an early passage to
Boston and the home environment of his friend. Thus the
highly trained and superbly gifted Lachaise, schooled in the
finest French sculpture tradition, became a participant in
the first heroic age of American art.

René Lalique, renowned decorative artist, jeweler, and
glassmaker took Lachaise on as a modeler, making and casting jewelry, designing vases and art nouveau ornaments. Lachaise made models in wax for casting in silver and gold,
and also carved in ivory and horn. He found the work "very

interesting" and was apparently very good at it. The art nouveau style of the period leaned toward exotic influences and Lachaise drew upon the sinuous forms of snakes, natural growths, and East Indian art for subject elements. In the approximately one year he worked for Lalique, Lachaise learned practical applications and techniques related to his classical training. Finally he ". . . had saved enough for a passage to America plus sixty dollars which I understood was to be possessed at landing—This being the only time where I have succeed to control my self for saving." [27]

Lachaise left France in December of 1905, never to return to his native land. He sailed from England on the S.S. *Ivernia* and arrived in Boston on January 13, 1906, with only thirty dollars in savings.

Boston and New York

Even though Lachaise had studied English at night school in Paris, he had no proficiency and had given it up as useless. He met a young man on the *Ivernia*, who troubled to introduce him to a family on Beacon Hill, with whom he found lodging.[28] His first job, Kirstein wrote with Lachaise' approval, was with a commercial sculptor named John Evans on Huntington Avenue in Boston. Assigned the execution of a Gothic Madonna he approached it with his Beaux-Arts' thoughtfulness and when he had nothing to show after a few days he was dismissed.[29] Another commentator refers to the Huntington Avenue job as having to do with cemetery gravestones.[30] Lachaise is reported by E. E. Cummings to have told of having been given an assignment to carve angels for a particular project, and when asked about his personal religious beliefs in relation to angels he replied that he didn't believe in them, causing his employer to fire him on the spot.[31]

Lachaise' landlady was acquainted with the prominent academic sculptor Henry Hudson Kitson and spoke to him at his offices in the Pope Building on Columbus Avenue and thereafter traveled to Quincy with her son to encourage Kitson's hiring of Lachaise in his studio practice. Kitson was then forty-one; he had been born in England and educated at the Beaux-Arts in Paris. He was working on a major Civil War memorial to the Confederate dead at Vicksburg, depicting soldiers, horses, and weaponry. Lachaise found himself unable to do his work swiftly enough for the demands of Kitson when called upon to do natural figures, but he turned to "moulding, casting guns, cartridge boxes, flags,

plaster architectural models" and felt he was ". . . beginning to make it." [32] In the spring he moved to a room in
Quincy on Johnson Avenue to reduce his commuting time.

"I happened to arrive at a period where the work was at a
rush and I would sleep at time few hours on the studio floor
with other workman for the convenience to our work regardless of Kitson's insistence to come to the house and sleep
there. . . ." [33] Lachaise worked at a variety of Civil War
monuments, often reduced to executing painstaking details
of uniform trimmings, belt buckles, buttons, epaulets, har-
nesses, and saddles for which he had been perhaps best prepared by his work with Lalique. Lachaise is reported to have
executed the "delicate tracery on the Irish Harp of Tara's
Muse" for the Fenway memorial to Patrick Andrew Collins
under Kitson's supervision. [34]

Later Lachaise wrote: "I landed in Boston. Life became
deeply wonderfull again. . . ." He then wrote of his Isabel,
whom he saw approximately twice a week, ". . . she has a
great deal of something which it's difficult for me to express
to you, something of a great calmness and ardour, a quality
of both old age and youth. . . ." He recognized that their
situation was not controllable, that there could be ". . . no
possible decisive solution for years to come," [35] so he turned
with renewed effort to his own work when he was not employed by Kitson and could not be with her.

He rented a studio at 110 Tremont Street, near Park,
across from a church, in an old studio building. There he
executed masks in honor of a friend's child, and did a bust
of Lincoln. [36] He reported to his Paris friend Cristophe, that
he was ". . . accumulating some sketches, letting them sit
for awhile and trying to clarify the expression. Sometimes
I go for six or seven months without feeling anything new,
but I think about my previous work, analyse it, looking for
landmarks, examining with a colder eye what was created in
moments of enthusiasm. Then there is *elimination*. I think
I'm in favorable circumstances at the moment. No foolish
work has to be done in order to eat. I have greater desires,
a thirst for conscientious work." [37]

At other moments Lachaise took time for recreation. In
the spring of 1906 he had taught himself to swim in Dor-
chester Bay, convenient to Quincy, ". . . and quickly liked
it so that I will swim a couple miles everyday." Often this
was around 11:00 P.M., when the tide was low. He found
that this regular exercise had a miraculous effect on his
health and energy, recalling that he had been rather delicate

in Europe.[38] From a somewhat frail figure, he developed a robustness of which he was so confident that he ". . . discarded and disdained any overcoat for . . . winter."[39] He also reported going fishing a few times in the Atlantic, enjoying the recreation, the beauty of the sea and coastline, and being tossed about on the waves in the sunshine.

A year later, reporting a stack of sketches and a newborn baby dozing (sculpture), he announced plans to send a bronze to the Salon in Paris, but that it would only be "15 centimeters high—Don't expect to see a mountain." He also wrote of a sculpture of a "nude reclining female—not finished." He recalled having spent two weeks in October 1907 with Isabel in Maine: "There I lived a great life . . . adventurous walks, sometimes having to cross some spots by swimming. It's almost uninhabited, and I hope go back next year . . . taking along camping equipment. . . ." "The sea is sometimes phosphorescent, and bathing in it at night becomes fantastic. A nude woman frolicking there is a marvelous thing. . . ."[40] At other points he mentions looking forward to tobogganing, searching for books, enjoying Aubrey Beardsley ("extraordinary, really great"), seeing Isadora Duncan a number of times: "In certain dances . . . she has reached the summit of that art form. I still remember one of her dances where the first of her movements gives you an enormous emotion which holds until the end of the dance. In her other dances I was only carried away in spots. This good, modest city Boston plans to prohibit her when she returns because she dances a bit too nude: as for myself, I feel that completely nude would be a beautiful thing, too. It's phenomenal how these virtuous and chaste people see nothing but sexes. . . ."[41]

At other times Lachaise would complain of his loneliness and separation from colleagues of common interest, "the old crew": ". . . sometimes I can hardly stand it, living almost all alone as I do, with the exception of (Isabel). No companions, no friends, only some forced relations due to work and daily life. What can I say to you, other than that dirty tricks and vileness make much of humanity; even so, I prefer the dirty tricks. The whole atmosphere is brutal, cynical and you can see right through people quickly, even though they're quite clever at their bluffs. . . ."[42]

"After my days work as an assistant I would work at night in a small studio of my own to my own work—Slowly personal expression came out of what I was so intensely living. This is where as reverently and with all the genuine simplicity possible I will express my profound gratitude to the leading inspiration which still leads me today, my wife—the majestic woman passed by once years ago by the Bank of the Seine. After several years in Boston I came to New York—my vision fully clear then." [43]

Isabel Nagle was born at Somerville, Massachusetts on May 2, 1872, the second daughter of Joseph Dutaud (1824) and Aurelie Gendron Dutaud both originally of the Province of Quebec, Canada.[44] She was christened Agloria P. Dutaud and was first married under that name. She and her older sister Adele spent most of their youth in Danvers, Massachusetts. Adele Dutaud (b. 1855) married Edward P. Pierce, a Massachusetts attorney who later became a Justice of the Supreme Judicial Court of Massachusetts. Adele's example apparently served as something of a model for the young Isabel, who married George B. Nagle, September 1, 1892, when she was twenty. The Pierce children were educated at least partially in France. Isabel would have been visiting her sister in France, while her own child Edward (b. June 1, 1893) was attending school, at the time she first encountered Gaston Lachaise.

Lachaise' reverence for Isabel was very great indeed. He felt moved repeatedly in his letters, public utterances, the "Comment," in *Creative Arts*, and the holographic autobiography to proclaim his "awakening" through this woman. It was during the Boston period that he worked both of the early versions of the *Reclining Couple*. So it was in Boston that the bold handling of the early standing women came about. Worked directly in clay or plasticene, roughly manipulated with wire and wood tools, those ten-inch figures of impressive scale, power, and dignity began to form themselves in the Tremont Street studio. It was the regal majesty of Isabel, her figure, and her inspiration that animated Lachaise' working procedures. The handling of these tiny figures surely owes something to the example of Rodin. But in the *Standing Woman*, 1910, the *Nude with Turban*, c. 1910 (Fig. 2), and the *Woman, Arms Akimbo*, 1910–12 (Fig. 4), there is a grandeur of scale, movement, and gusto that goes beyond even the Parisian master. This was surely what Lachaise meant when he said that "slowly personal expression came out of what I was so intensely living." He was ready to show these vigorous, life-like, passionate figures which were to be so shocking, compelling, and disturbing to a generation. He had prepared himself so that he was ready when the occasion should arise. The first occasion, of course, would be the celebrated Armory Show of 1913 and he would have to move to New York to meet that challenge.

Kitson found his practice expanding and he felt the need to relocate in New York City. He wanted Lachaise to continue work on the Vicksburg Memorial in Quincy and to join him in New York upon its completion. Lachaise had to decide whether to separate himself from Isabel by so many miles. His decision was complicated by his contempt for Kitson's work, which he told Isabel was ". . . dishonest . . . and absolutely of no use to the world." [45] Nevertheless both he and Isabel had discussed the problem of fostering his career, and they both recognized that the future of a serious sculptor lay in the marketplace city. Lachaise knew that he required a period of subsidy in which to establish a foothold in Manhattan. In 1912 he did move to New York to work in the MacDougal Alley studio Kitson had rented in Greenwich Village. Lachaise found lodgings in a boarding house on Washington Square South which was adequate if not overly large and there he began his life-sized figure of Isabel.

Arthur B. Davies and Gutzon Borglum visited Kitson's studio in MacDougal Alley to discuss an international art show to be held at the 69th Regiment Armory, Lexington Avenue at 25th Street, New York City. Hearing of the proposed exhibition, Lachaise asked Kitson's permission to show the visitors his work, one of which was invited (in plaster) to the landmark exhibition of the following year. That meeting with Arthur B. Davies was only the first of many meetings and Davies came to enjoy Lachaise' company and to value his judgment concerning his own work. [46]

Lachaise is said to have looked for work with Paul Manship and been turned down. [47] When approached to teach sculpture to a "mad poet" from his boarding house, Lachaise took the man to Manship's studio where the poet was likewise turned away, but on this occasion Manship invited Lachaise to come back the next day and there would be work for him. [48] From the letters to Isabel it can be seen, even though they are undated, that Lachaise worked for a time with both Kitson and Manship, occasionally taking a prolonged holiday for his own work. Before long the Kitson work was terminated and Lachaise worked for Manship on very much the same basis he had established with Kitson, ranging from a regular workday to twelve and more hours a day and alternating with unpaid vacations devoted to his own work. "I worked intensively both for a living—with extra hours time on account of need of extra money for living and producing my own work (as required). I would work long stretches of at time 12 hours as an assistant to Paul Manship. . . ."[49] Lachaise' experiences at the Beaux-Arts, with Lalique and with Kitson, all came to use in his work for Manship. He was called upon to do a variety of neoclassic styled carvings and to perform technical processes requiring considerable skill. He carved ornaments like leaves and fruit, pedestals, and detailing where necessary. He was given the job of transferring surface qualities to the stone in portraits—textures of skin and the like. He thus worked on the Manship head of John D. Rockefeller, Sr., and participated in the work on the J. Pierpont Morgan Memorial placed in the Metropolitan Museum of Art. He worked on the model and the stone tablet, which he carved alone.

Paul Manship, then the darling of official sculptors, had studied at the Art Students League, worked for a summer with Solon Borglum, and attended the Pennsylvania Academy before winning a Prix de Rome. He became interested in preclassical and classical antiquity upon which he depended for models, themes, and treatments. He was three years younger than Lachaise, born in St. Paul, Minnesota in 1885. His practice was so successful that he needed assistance and Lachaise brought a variety of talents and experience difficult to find in the New York of that day. The Manships treated Lachaise well, introducing him to patrons and visitors of distinction in a most respectful manner. Lachaise' letters to Isabel often reflect the Manships' kindnesses to him, their travel together, and dinners shared with people of fashion:

Worked all day on the bas relief. Manship likes it and after looking at it a long time Faulkner concluded "It is wonderful." Manship telephoned me to go to a tea at some Mrs. Goodyear's. Met a French-Swiss dancer there. Invited to go to a concert tomorrow. You know how brilliant I am among people—It is courageous (of them) to support me.[50]

Lachaise' separation from Isabel was not easy for either of them. He most urgently wanted her to join him in New York and for them to marry. At this time and always thereafter, whenever they were separated, he would write at least once every day, expressing his devotion, describing his work and other activities, and anything she would be likely to enjoy— the botanical gardens, the aquarium, mountain climbing in Vermont, seeing Mazarin in *Electra*, attending a Chaplin movie, going to Coney Island to swim, seeing Pavlova, examining the Greek painted vases at the Metropolitan, or viewing a Mexican bullfight movie. He waited anxiously upon her approval. Oftentimes his letters to Isabel comforted and encouraged her in the ordeal of their separation, her ethical and emotional problems in the marriage, and her duty to her son:

Your life is like that—you cannot be other than you are. You are the result of all your thoughts, feelings, so be calm in face of every-thing that must come. If your son grows old intelligently he will understand. If you attain to loving a person you do not take possession of them but give them as much liberty as possible—even to the sacrifice of yourself. He is young but many men are also like that. I hope that he will change, that he will understand. Speak to him. Be calm and strong. Tell me when I can write or come to you.[51]

With the outbreak of the war, Lachaise' thoughts in his letters to Isabel reflect growing concern for his mother and sister then in Paris. Subsequent letters reflect telegrams, changes of plans, complex bookings on ships, and eventual success in securing passage to America. Lachaise' disdain for the European war, the waste and needless conflict, is repeatedly underscored in his letters to Isabel.

For me the proclamation of neutrality of the U.S. compels all people within the U.S. to stand aloof.

. . . (the) paper says you can hear the cannon—Poor savage idiots! About me—all is well, even without naturalization. I have the 1st paper—have to wait 2 years for the rest. I am very sad for my sister. My mother—its the 2nd war she has seen. The poor devils in Europe —why not revolt—finish with this war and unite. If that could happen it would be worth something. But in the meantime what low savagery—Flag—country—honor—glory God—all these belong to the militarist.[52]

Many letters recount his loneliness—"No letter from you today. I waited for each post—nothing this evening again— all the hours until morning to wait. I saw Davies—dined with him—I worked on your statuette all afternoon. I would like you to see it. I don't know whether you will like it. . . ." And later he writes of examining her two little black slippers in the evening in the studio, writes of their roundness from her being—". . . I worked from you all afternoon expressing your body—expressing your thoughts—your body is your thought. It has been burning hot in the studio—it is a good atmosphere around me—I am all aflame—a flame which burns of you. The heat, the light in the studio, the work, the little slippers, the 4 corners of the studio close me in with you." Later he added, "You are long in coming, the time is frightfully long. I worked Sunday—happy hours—I was near you. I received a few lines from you . . . was a profound joy. . . ." [53]

Edward Nagle entered Harvard in 1913 and would with normal progress have graduated in 1917, but he dropped out in his third year. His experiences at Harvard had been very favorable, falling in with John Dos Passos, E. E. Cummings, and a number of the young men surrounding the *Harvard Monthly*, including James Sibley Watson, Jr., Gilbert Seldes, and Robert Hillyer. With his French educational experience, wide ranging interests in literature and art, and his special insight gained through his mother and Lachaise, Nagle was an influential person at least in opening doors for his fellow students. "Nagle introduced us to the world of the modern. . . . It was Nagle who infected both Cummings and me with the excitements and experiments of the school of Paris. In the arts everything was abolished. Everything must be reinvented from scratch. It was in Nagle's room that I first saw copies of *Blast*, with Eliot's early poems. . . ." [54]

In 1916 Lachaise achieved his naturalization as an American citizen, writing to Isabel, ". . . was an idiot not to have done it long ago." [55] With Edward in college and the citizenship established, Gaston and Isabel began to work for her divorce. In later years, Isabel recalled, "Lachaise was wonderful in his waiting, saying 'What will give you the greatest happiness is what I want' and 'Your happiness is the first thing in my life' and 'I work through you.' " [56] At this point Lachaise had been a United States resident for over ten years. Isabel recalled a poem they had both enjoyed and took turns in reading to each other:

> The days of distance and the nights apart
> Are at an end,
> All the long lonely winter of the heart
> Is at an end;
> Our grief is ended and our joys begun
> We have climbed the night
> At last we reach the sun!
>
> —HAFIZ

Lachaise wrote in the war years to Isabel, saying, "I went to see Guthrie (his attorney). He told me that (George Nagle) would give her the divorce by furnishing evidence against him but that naturally it was understood that she would not demand alimony. . . . He said it would take 3 months for the first divorce paper—and 6 months after that before remarrying. He said it would be simple and easy and it would so help to clear the air." [57]

An exchange of poems in the middle teens reflects the depth and continuity of Isabel's [58] and Gaston's [59] love, perhaps as long as fifteen years after they had first met. In fact, a Certificate of Marriage was found in Mme. Lachaise' papers recording that Gaston and Isabel Nagel (sic) were married on the 25th of June 1917 at the office of the City Clerk of the Borough of Manhattan.[60] The Lachaise wedding supper was hosted by Manship. It was a time of fulfillment for both Lachaise and Isabel as well as the end of a long trial for each of them. Lachaise never failed to record his devotion to Isabel and the role she played in his life and art as his "primary inspiration." [61]

In Lachaise' own words in Boston, ". . . slowly personal expression came out." Then in New York, ". . . my vision fully clear then . . . ," he was prepared to work. Once the problems of living were resolved—his mother's permanent installation in New York, Edward's placement at Harvard, naturalization, and finally marriage to Isabel—he began producing his own work in some fullness. By 1917, ". . . After having completed some twenty pieces of sculpture—marble carving and bronze—and also a life-size figure in plaster—'Woman,'" he was ready to think of arranging for a one-man show in the galleries of New York:

I beguin to make the turn of the galleries existing at the time—trying to interest one of the Art Dealer for a one man show—some of them came to my studio—among them some liked my work, but that was all—One of the most successful salesman of the period came to look over my sculptures and concluded in a very gracefully toned voice—"You have done beautifully"—"You have done more beautifully than anyone else—but, I do not like your type of figures," with that sentence I was "out of questions" as for my good salesman concern. . . .

After trying unsuccessfully some more Galleries which by the way have bought my work since for their personal collection—I was left with but two more chances—reserved to the last as the more serious and important one—"291" and the Bourgeois Gallery. I stepped to 291 which was very familiar to me, being there a devoted visitor, I addressed Mr. Stieglitz for the first time, asking, if he would be interested to see some of my work—My question some what went wrong—bringing out from Mr. Stieglitz, the argument, "How can I know if I will be interested without having see your work?" I got impatient take my hat and left. I was, several years later (invited) to be Mr. Stieglitz guest with a one man show exhibition in the Intimate Galleries in Park Avenue. After this incident, only my last chance was left.

I appeared at the Bourgeois Galleries—unwrapping without a word a piece of my sculpture before Mr. Bourgeois, and waited—Mr. Bourgeois looked over my think (sic) for over five minutes I managed to keep quiet—"I like it" came Mr. Bourgeois words—"You want an exhibition? I will come to your studio tomorrow morning and see the rest." Mr. Bourgeois was there early the next morning in is way to his Gallery.

When he left, very cordial and cherfull he told me—"I will send you this afternoon a letter to confirm the arrangement concerning your coming exhibition in my Gallery."

I was radiant, running down Fifth Avenue to our small apartment to tell at last the great news to my wife—this was indeed a joy to her generous devotion to me. I then rushed to my bread earning occupation as Manship's assistant.

Money was to be needed to carry to full completion the work to be exhibited—and also more freedom of time for it—these two things rather conflicing. I found the only way out was to increase in one side my working hours time as an assistant, for money, and sleep less of the remaining time to carry my own work.

I did that very cheerfully for the next few month until the opening of my show, which raised great interest but small cash—my only alternative then was to keep going at the same rate at my two jobs for several years to come. Going up to "bed" at four in the morning on a small cot in the studio. I would read for one hour by a glaring electric light some of my book would be Stefanshon Life in the North, Amundsen, and Scott in the Antartic. These men were my hero, and I read them exhilerated by the comfort of my little cot, relaxing warmly until 8 at the morning—to get up again for assistant work. My own work beguin to sale—few persons very entousiasm from the beginning multiplied to more numerous collectors, they where never of the frivolous type, but very strong in their appreciation. My "assistant" activity was eventually dropped and all of my time devoted to my own work.[62]

Bourgeois remembered the day of the meeting to be in 1916 and he recalled that the exhibition was first scheduled for 1917 and was then later rescheduled for February 1918. Lachaise' studio was on Twelfth street at the time and they visited back and forth in the studio and at the gallery at 668 Fifth Avenue. Bourgeois recognized in their visits and conversations that Lachaise "had a philosophy—a real insight into womankind." [63] The exhibition when it was finally mounted consisted of twenty-nine sculptural pieces plus drawings. There were Peacocks, dolphins, sea lions, two busts, a number of small statuettes of female figures, reliefs, and the patined plaster life-sized figure of Isabel. Bourgeois told Lachaise that the works must have names. Lachaise replied "anything you want," and the titles *Pudeur, La Force Eternelle* (Fig. 6), *Rhythme, Amazone, Summer Clouds* were given. The life-sized figure of Isabel was titled *Elevation* (Fig. 17).

Reception for the exhibition was generally positive. Five New York daily papers and one magazine published reviews and, while all were favorable, only Henry McBride in *The Sun* found the work outstanding. The vitality and force of the pieces were acknowledged, but the artist's muse was considered to be unsightly and overweight by most commentators. Daniel Chester French, the dean of official sculptors at the time told Bourgeois: "His vision is monstrous, how can you show these things?" The dealer remembered French ". . . as shaking with rage, he was so shocked by Lachaise' sculpture." [64]

The slender ideal of American wartime womanhood was no doubt a far cry from the full blown figure of Isabel. Nonetheless a number of sculptures sold, one to a Mrs. Josiah Oliver Wolcott, wife of the Delaware Senator, who was initially disturbed by the *Elevation*. Bourgeois told her the story of Mme. Litvine, humble old singer of the Paris Opera, who invoked laughter from the audience when she made her stage entrance. "After four bars of Beethoven, that woman arose to an ascendant stature and the whole house was mesmerized. When she sang the audience was lost. She became a goddess." Mrs. Wolcott, who had expressed horror at the "fat woman," recognized the ascendant quality of *Elevation* instantaneously and responded, "My God! It's great!"

Writing at a later time, Henry McBride recalled his first experience of *Elevation:*

. . . it was in a specially wakeful moment that I sauntered into the old Bourgeois Gallery of a dozen years ago and came upon the Lachaise sculptures there exposed. Whatever there was in me of Vasari sprang instantly into the quick. I felt, "Here's business for the historian. This is great" . . . What astonished me most with its beauty was a female nude that may or may not have been larger than life but seemed so. There was an air of exuberance, of exaltation, of expansiveness, about the figure that meant only one thing. The carving represented an ideal. This ideal was not the usual one. In fact the usualness of the usual ideal had been for a long time the special trait that critics in America had most contended with. This one had nothing to do with fashion, nothing to do with the sort of thing that is taught in schools. To eyes that had grown somewhat habituated to the platitudinous carvings of the day the Lachaise "Woman" was so different that at first she seemed a priestess from another planet than this. She must have been at least early-Egyptian, early-Arabian, or at least pre-Greek! But that was only at first. In a minute or two the strangeness disappeared, the authoritative satisfaction of the sculptor in his work made itself felt and a mere critic could see a beauty that though new was dateless and therefore as contemporary as it was "early." I left the gallery firmly convinced I had seen a masterpiece.[65]

Lachaise continued his work as an assistant to Manship, working as he could at his own pieces, drawing on his muse, exhibiting from time to time at the Society of Independent Artists in 1918 and 1919, at the Penguin Club, and at the First Annual of American Painters, Sculptors and Gravers. A number of young college chums from Edward Nagle's Harvard years were introduced to Lachaise, who was already very much a celebrity to them. In particular E. E. Cummings and his sidekick from the French concentration camp—William Slater Brown—found Lachaise an exciting person. While Mme. Lachaise had expressed her objections to the "arty" titles of the works in the Bourgeois show, Cummings quoted Lachaise as saying: "Ai don lai kit ai hay tit 'pudeur' dat means something to me dirty . . ."[66] in a letter to his mother in Cambridge. At another point he described *Elevation*, ". . . his six foot plaster nude which it took him three years says Edward Nagle to build, which he twice completement demolished. . . ."[67]

Cummings was finishing up his *Enormous Room* for publication, enjoying New York City, its night life, aquarium, burlesque houses, and finding that many of his Harvard acquaintances were now relocating in the city. The endeavors of Scofield Thayer (Fig. 37) and James Sibley Watson, Jr. (Fig 30) to recreate *The Dial* magazine, were exciting and commendable to him. While Nagle introduced him to Lachaise, it was Cummings who brought Lachaise to the attention of Thayer and Watson and subsequently the magazine's staff. In early 1919 Cummings wrote from New York to his mother saying, ". . . I sleep with Lachaise in his studio. . . ."[68] It was Cummings who selected *Dusk* (Fig. 59), the bronze plaque for the frontispiece of the January 1, 1920 number of *The Dial*.[69] Knowing that Lachaise was soon to have his second one-man show at Bourgeois January 31 through February 21, 1920, Cummings arranged with Thayer to do a substantial article on Lachaise' sculpture for the

February number of the magazine. Cummings was a victim of his very youth and its exasperation with unfriendly criticism; his attack began on page 194 and continued through 204—a celebration, panegyric, devastating attack on Lachaise' "critics" and roundhouse knockout punch to all competitors, national or international:

. . . Lachaise has, in the past few years, made a large number of artists extremely enthusiastic, and a great many gallerygoers very nervous, not to mention the ladies and gentlemen who may have died of anger. But the official "critics," perhaps realizing the disastrous consequences to "criticism" of a genuine reaction on their part to work of overwhelming aesthetic value, have as it were agreed to risk nothing. An exception which proves the rule is Mr. McBride of The Sun, who on Sunday (February 17, 1918) said, in the course of some hair-raising platitudes, "I like this statue (The Elevation) immensely."

Three things Lachaise, to any one who knows him, is, and is beyond the shadow of a doubt: inherently naif, fearlessly intelligent, utterly sincere. It is accurate to say that his two greatest hates are the hate of insincerity and the hate of superficiality. That Lachaise is supremely and incorrigibly enthusiastic about his adopted country would appear (in the light of that country's treatment of him) perfectly unreasonable, had it not its reverse side, which is the above mentioned disgust with superficiality and contempt for insincerity—two qualities which he attributes in a high degree to his native land. As his work proves, he has no use for prettiness. This work of his, a crisp and tireless searching for the truths of nature as against the facts of existence, negates incidentally, as Cezanne's solid strivings incidentally negate Monet.

Lachaise's work is the absolutely authentic expression of a man very strangely alive.

Every one has read, and no one has heard him boast, that he "studied at the Ecole des Beaux-Arts 1898–1903, exhibited at the Salon des Artistes Français 1899, worked with Lalique and Aube 1901," took various prizes, and so forth. What no one knows, outside his immediate friends, with whom he is preternaturally frank, is Lachaise's attitude toward triumphs which would have seduced a mind less curiously and originally sensitive. The fact is that he regards them with something between amusement and disgust. This is not a question of modesty, but of direct and fearless thinking—at which, as has been already stated, Lachaise is a past master. . . .

To the vocal gesture which preceded grammar Lachaise is completely sensitive. Consequently, in his enormous and exquisite way, Lachaise negates OF with IS. To say that the 1918 exhibition at the Bourgeois Galleries drew from the "critics" more statements of ungentle unintelligence, and from the gallery-going public more expressions of enthusiastic ignorance, than any one-man show of sculpture previously held on the Avenue, is but to do justice to all concerned, including Monsieur Bourgeois. The Elevation, which as we have already noted, occasioned, in the case of Mr. McBride, the sole unbiased reaction of "criticism" to this exhibition, was responsible for, on the one hand, more unclever exasperation and on the other more fulsome ecstasy than all the rest of the show put together. Lest any should accuse us of hyperbole, we will quote a sample of each. . . .

The reason why all official and unofficial "criticism" OF The Elevation fails and fails so obviously as in the specimens quoted is this: The Elevation is not a noun, but a "modern statue," not a statue OF Something or Some One BY a man named Gaston Lachaise—but a complete tactile self-orchestration, a magnificently conjugating largeness, an IS. The Elevation may not be declined: it should not and cannot be seen; it must be heard: heard as a super-Wagnerian poem of flesh, a gracefully colossal music. In mistaking The Elevation for a noun the "critics" did something superhumanly asinine. In creating The Elevation as a verb Lachaise equalled the dreams of the very great artists of all time. . . .

The exhibition at the Fifth Avenue gallery consisted of sixteen sculptures and fourteen drawings. Bourgeois published a four page catalog with his own essay and reproductions of *Elevation* and the *Love* group (Figs. 17, 88). The latter sculpture, in plaster, over life size, consisted of a standing male figure, carrying a woman lifted to his shoulders. The plaster was later destroyed, according to Henry McBride, when Lachaise was being put out of one of his studios for failure to pay rent. Bourgeois considered it Lachaise' greatest work, and he wrote of it quite ecstatically in the preface to the 1920 catalog.

Lachaise on receiving an advance copy of the text for *The Dial* piece by Cummings went to the West Fourteenth Street apartment only to find Cummings out. He left a note in the keyhole:

> Couming.
> That great very great—may I just say that now
> I will say as I can fully when I see you—
> We all say the same at home—
>
> LACHAISE

And hardly had Brown and I finished reading it when in came Lachaise, to whom the is it seventy four stairs—I forget what you told me—were apparently as nothing—or I should say two times seventy four, since this was the second time he'd climbed to see me. He was appreciative as only Lachaise can be appreciative—you who met him at Joe's can imagine how (much) that means to anyone. Then he produced the essay, showed me some terribly obvious blunders, with the words and then we drank tea and ate buttered toast, discussing the critical world in general and, with the essay as a basis, in particular. Then Lachaise said "I should run," and we wished one another good night. I plead guilty to feeling excessively happy.[70]

Critical comment other than that of Cummings varied in the New York and Philadelphia papers, but there was invariably a tone of serious consideration accorded to the work. Only Hamilton Easter Field and McBride were without reserve in their praise. There were no sales from the show, and new debts had been incurred. High sales expectations combined with the disapproval Mme. Lachaise had expressed toward Bourgeois' "purple prose" in the preface to the catalog resulted in Lachaise' eventual withdrawal from the gallery.

Lachaise had the feeling that he could work with C. W. Kraushaar then at 680 Fifth Avenue and he began to do so shortly after his break with Bourgeois. Bourgeois remained loyal to Lachaise throughout his life, often listing him as his chief discovery. He said of him, "Lachaise was impractical . . . as an artist should be . . . he should never have married . . . Lachaise was an uncompromising man. . . ." [71]

Kraushaar represented Lachaise well for a number of years and was agreeable to the artist's use of his Fifth Avenue window to show new works to the world in the nature of a newsreel commentary on what was happening in the Lachaise studio. Bourgeois understood that Kraushaar had loaned Lachaise $10,000 against future sales at the time that Lachaise withdrew from his gallery. Bourgeois claimed that even with that handsome advance Lachaise continued to sell directly out of his studio to collectors and even occasionally to a dealer.[72]

The exhibitions at Bourgeois had the effect of bringing the artist to a larger audience. Manship was going abroad and, perhaps since he could not undertake the work for the frieze over the elevator core doorways in the new American Telephone and Telegraph Building, Lachaise received the commission. Bourgeois expressed the view that he, Senator Wolcott's wife, and possibly Arthur B. Davies had helped Lachaise' candidacy. The frieze is a joyful piece of carving in lightly grained marble and animated by grace and feeling, in remarkable contrast to the earlier twin building's treatment. This $20,000 commission put official sculptors on notice that Lachaise was a competitor of the utmost seriousness. Another commission that came from the Bourgeois arrangement was for an Arch of Triumph at Madison and Twenty-fifth Streets for the American troops to march through on their return from France.[73]

Lachaise did flat reliefs in plaster and/or papier mâché which were said to be decorative and effective. But although the artist had been exposed to the ways of society in his association with Manship and his entertaining and charming of men of influence as a fellow man-of-the-world, Lachaise was not skillful in dealing with the men who provided commissions and he seldom received the success which his technical and aesthetic abilities warranted.

Isabel Lachaise had spent much of her childhood and adolescence in Massachusetts and New England, and that climate had a sense of rightness to her. Her first husband's sister Daisy had a summer place in Maine and Isabel and George Nagle visited her at the "camp" in Georgetown. Later George and Isabel bought a small summer house across the road from his sister.[74] Lachaise expressed pleasure in fishing, especially at the ocean and in the beauty of coastal walks and boating, in letters to his old studio mate, Christophe, in 1907–8.[75] He loved the light on the water, the movement of the waves and spoke of his "passion for the sea" and swimming.

In 1908 Gaston and Isabel spent two weeks in Maine, and Lachaise wrote of it, ". . . a marvelous state, the sea, a coastline of rocks with forests, especially firs, which begin right with the rocks and all along the coast, groups of islands of all shapes, but always rocky and generally covered with firs shouldering each other."[76]

After their marriage, Isabel and Gaston spent some vacation periods in Woodstock, New York, and evidently had enjoyable visits there. Lachaise wrote rhapsodically of climbing mountains and of the "European atmosphere, the falls on all sides, the little forest and the brooks."[77] Hart Crane chronicles a splendid Thanksgiving party at which he, Slater Brown, Edward Nagle, Gaston and Isabel Lachaise, and others cooked, ate and drank, danced madly to jazz records until exhausted.[78] Though she was not unhappy in Woodstock, Isabel preferred Maine and in 1922 they began to look for a property in that state. By 1923 work was going ahead on the renovation of the Georgetown, Maine, house which they had bought. They eventually acquired, perhaps in three stages, the house and general store which became a studio over the water, a lot at Indian Point, to which

they walked for picnics in the evening twilight, and one of
those small islands which Lachaise admired. It is uncertain
when they actually moved into the house in its finished state,
but Hart Crane wrote in May 1925 to his mother saying:

The Lachaises are soon to leave for their country place near Bath,
Maine, and have been nice enough to urge me to an extended visit
with them this summer if I can possibly do so. Just a mile from the
ocean—and a wonderful beach set in a cove of rocks topped by pines!
How I would love to go—[79]

In Marsden Hartley's words, the Lachaise summer place
was, "A house of the middle '70s . . . (the) usual two room
length front and a long ell to the eastward providing room
after room. . . ." He went on to describe the garden and the
roses, ". . . pink ramblers of several hues." Hartley was
himself a State-of-Mainer and he loved the landscape and
the coastal views as Lachaise did. He was a friend of both
the Lachaises and corresponded consistently with Isabel after
her husband's death. He wrote of "The studio of Gaston Lachaise overhanging the Tidal River at Robin Hood Cove,
Georgetown, Maine . . . (and of) fine old sign posts point to
three pleasing destinations, with the names of Five Islands,
Little River and Indian Point." [80]

Each late Spring Isabel would travel to Maine with her
maid and supervise the freshening up of the house. A great
deal of painting, pruning, and preparing would be carried
out and the house shone with a stylish concern for details.
Paintings by Marin, Gleizes, Weber, Kuniyoshi, Stella, and
other leading contemporaries were displayed along with
works by Lachaise. Furniture tended to be New England
originals and the rugs were handhooked masterpieces which
rivaled the paintings. Ample bookcases fairly bulged with a
collection of catholic literary taste in both French and English but with an emphasis on the new direction in advanced
and experimental literature.

Lachaise was happy in his house and workshop and even
planned that one day he would spend most of the year in
Maine. He designed the cellar and built it with William
Zorach's help, reworked the house and its porches, and had
drafted plans for a garage. He loved the flowers and worked
in the garden, planting, weeding, developing an elaborate
rose garden arrangement and the terracing with John Thi-
bodeau, the handyman, chauffeur, gardener.[81] "He would
very often bring Madame Lachaise flowers in the city even
when they didn't have food." [82] An early riser, he often

fixed her breakfast and brought it to her bedside with one perfect flower on the tray.

In the early twenties Lachaise became a member of the Independent Society of Artists and then one of its directors, along with Walter Pach, John Sloan, Gertrude Whitney, Robert Henri, and others of similar importance. Lachaise was elected to the position and served for a number of years. Eventually he broke with Pach at a public meeting of the group when Pach denounced American artists and lauded the French. Lachaise defended the Americans, contending that Pach was using the organization for his personal publicity purposes. In a fury Lachaise resigned from the Society as did Hamilton Easter Field. At no other time did the sculptor associate himself with an artist's professional or social organization.[83]

In subsequent years Lachaise spent a great deal of time soliciting commissions from architects and influential members of commissioning groups, making and presenting sketches and models for architectural projects. In his 1924 essay Gallatin wrote:

The most important full-length image Lachaise has executed is a study for an heroic figure intended to be placed in the Telegraph and Telephone Building on Broadway. If the directors of this company decide to have this project carried out, the figure, after still further simplifications, would be cut in marble and stand about twenty-two feet high. Placed in the vast and imposing room which forms the ground floor of this building, against a marble wall and facing the principal entrance, viewed through a vista of columns, the statue would be seen to great advantage. In this superb creation of Lachaise's the serene figure of the young woman, classic in its simplicity, and full of grace, is seen holding in one hand a globe of the world, while in the other rest several towering skyscrapers, which have become symbolical of New York. . . .[84]

Lachaise did cement plaques for architect Welles Bosworth's house on Long Island, and a life size marble figure for the Atkinson Allen estate. He executed Zodiac designs for the elevator doors of the building on the Northwest corner of Seventh Avenue at Thirty-ninth Street and a peacock for the James Deering estate. He received the Coast Guard Memorial commission, a spread-winged seagull installed at Arlington Cemetery, and in the thirties he received two commissions for Rockefeller Center, a commission for the 1933 World's Fair in Chicago, and he was working on perhaps the most important and potentially significant commission of his life when he died in 1935—the free standing male and

female figures on either side of a marble cylinder symbolizing "Welcoming the Peoples." The energy spent on obtaining
these paltry orders and the negligible importance of their
"public sculpture" qualities when compared with the artist's
own seriousness and high art purpose, make it very clear
that Lachaise was his own best patron, and his time was best
spent following his own need to express himself rather than
pursuing commissions from custodians of common-denomi-
nator taste. Kirstein wrote in the 1935 monograph: ". . . it is
illuminating to consider him, an acknowledged artist of su-
perior talent, in relation to one factor that qualifies this kind
of recognition—economic security. Lachaise is not represented in the Metropolitan Museum of Art nor in many other
American museums. Until this year, and the commission for
the Fairmount Park Memorial in Philadelphia, Lachaise
has had to wait for a public monument worthy of his talents." [85] Lachaise himself, writing in 1928 said, ". . . to
the business man . . . the dollar evaluation is the sole spiritual criterion when faced by an artist with his work. . . .
They consider him awkward, timid, unworldly, strange, etc.
etc. Yet they fall easily for charlatans." [86]

To be sure, Lachaise pursued his work, did portraits of
artists and writers of distinction, and of children, executed
the Rockefeller Tomb at Tarrytown, spent endless hours seeking commissions, produced some popular successes—such
as his peacock sculptures for Brook Green Gardens—and for
a number of Long Island estates, made animal and bird
sculptures of charm and easy aesthetic currency, created
radiator caps in the form of turkeys or bumble bees, and even
did a "portrait" of a race horse. He kept busy, working,
producing his own works, caring for his beloved Isabel,
maintaining her apartment in the Brevoort, the Grosvenor,
or elsewhere, his studio at whatever location it might be, and
his single bedroom with its glaring light and minimal con-
veniences. In addition he supported the house in Georgetown,
Maine, and sent money religiously to Edward Nagle, his
wife's son. He became obsessed with the problems of his
life, the money management. He would have a success, receive a large check, distribute it to his various commitments
and be penniless again within days. At such times, requiring
still more money for Isabel, his own work, for rent bills,
for Nagle's psychoanalysis, he would pawn a sculpture or
sell a sheaf of drawings to E. Weyhe for a fraction of their
market value. He was even known to pawn his sculpture
tools at a point of special desperation.

It is instructive to realize that Lachaise created every major sculpture of his life, with but one exception, as his own work and devotion to his own ideal, without support for either labor or materials. The *Elevation* (Fig. 17), the *Floating Woman* (Fig. 67), the *Heroic Woman* (Fig. 22), *The Man* (Fig. 46), *Dans la Nuit* (Fig. 87), were all produced on the speculation that they would be admired and perhaps brought to final form through the enthusiasm of a collector or institutional patron. The very reason that the *Standing Woman* 1912–27, took so long to complete was that the casting in bronze had to be paid from earnings—from fountains, architectural commissions, and more trivial work—and thus the piece, while finished for the 1918 show at Bourgeois, languished for nearly a decade before it could appear in its intended material. The daily letters written by Lachaise to Isabel chronicle an endless run of borrowings, advances, efforts at sales, checks being sent now with a bit more to follow later in the day or perhaps tomorrow, telegraphed money orders, excuses and hopes for tomorrow or the day after. Isabel kept every letter, and there is often a simple eloquence to the description of the sculptor's efforts, his long hours at his art and the painful waste of his time in securing a few dollars here, sitting in architects' offices there, waiting for phone calls or letters that seem forever bottled up in bureaucratic committee decisions, approvals, and late payments.

The twenties are often thought of as nostalgic good old days of support for the arts and high achievement in literature, painting and sculpture, music and theatre. They were also difficult days. Cummings remembers Scofield Thayer "... suffering a martyrdom, a perfect battle month to month to keep *The Dial* magazine running ..." during the early and middle twenties.[87] Lachaise told Reuben Nakian that Stefan Bourgeois offered Roman sculptures to friends of Lachaise who wanted to see Lachaise sculptures in the Fifth Avenue gallery.[88] Nakian also remembers that Lachaise told him Kraushaar used Lachaise sculptures in the window to bring patrons into the gallery only to try to sell them old master drawings and paintings. Nakian recalls that on one occasion Lachaise made an exact duplicate of the Demeter and Kore, stone relief of the Musée d'Eleusis in order to make money from some wealthy man who wished to have the piece.

Speaking many years later, Madame Lachaise recalled, "If I had been the frugal, careful type that they (his family) were, we wouldn't have gotten along. . . ." "Lachaise had no understanding of money—it was all crumpled up in his pockets, merely a means of getting something, not to keep. He always had a quality of grace, never depressed . . . One evening we were penniless and he had gone off to the Valentine Gallery to raise some money. He came back with a good smile and threw his hands out of his pockets and bills showered over the bed, saying, 'Now we'll go out and have a good meal.' " [89]

The Dial

The Dial magazine of the twenties was a literary journal with a tradition, owned and edited by a remarkable pair of ex-*Harvard Monthly* editors with money and a shared mission to educate the literate American public concerning the state of current plastic arts and literature. Scofield Thayer (Fig. 37) had been a student of Santayana at Harvard, had contributed writings to the 1916–19 *Dial*, as had his colleague James Sibley Watson, who had graduated from Harvard in 1916, three years later than Thayer. Both young men had been supporters of the *Little Review* and had joined in favor of James Joyce in the fight over the right to have *Ulysses* printed. They were both interested in publishing, in Freud, in the course of contemporary literature, and in the remarkable development of what was then called "modern art." Their concern for publishing from the *Monthly* through their own post-Harvard writing for little magazines brought them to the point of purchasing a seventy-five per cent interest in *The Dial* in 1919 in order to re-create it as a vehicle for the publication of the best writing of their time and the best art of the emerging modern movement. It was their conviction that both European and American writers and artists should be seen together in order to best serve the evolving taste of the American intellectual world.

In its first incarnation *The Dial* served as the organ of the Transcendentalists 1840–44, with Margaret Fuller and Emerson as editors and Oliver Wendell Holmes and Hawthorne as contributors. The magazine was revived in 1880 in Chicago by Francis F. Browne, but in 1916–17 it was moved to New York City under the direction of Martyn Johnson and editorial policy shifted before long from that of a literary monthly in the genteel end-of-century tradition to that of a companion of *The New Republic* and *The Nation* operating in the arena of social humanitarianism. Like many of the "little magazines" of the period, *The Dial* under its new editor

George Bernard Donlin showed a concern with social issues, politics, feminism, negro rights, and pacifism with such contributors as Randolph Bourne, John Dewey, Harold Laski and Thorstein Veblen. *The Dial* of the twenties under Thayer and Watson chose to remove itself from "fumy politics" and to pursue an independent role as a standard of international criticism, committed to reviewing the most significant books, and to reproducing advanced works of art. *The Dial* was an aesthetic journal—committed to the belief "that art is satisfying and meaningful primarily as form, as a concrete and vivid organization of human experience." [90] They sought to establish a new method of literary criticism, based on the structure and technique of the work. *The Dial*'s influence has surely been in the development, encouragement, and proliferation of the concept of close textual analysis related to what has come to be known as "the new criticism"— a formalist attitude in the criticism of the arts. The writings of Remy de Gourmont, Ezra Pound, and T. S. Eliot led to this philosophic position. A number of writers for earlier little magazines like *The Little Review, Poetry,* and *Others,* including Ezra Pound, H.D., Richard Aldington, Amy Lowell and William Carlos Williams came to offer work to *The Dial,* which became the prototype of American little magazines.[91]

With Watson as publisher, Thayer became editor, charting the course of aestheticism, devotion to "the best in all of the arts . . . in both the new and the old created in America side by side with . . . the new and the old produced abroad." [92] From its first issue under the new leadership the journal sought to be as deeply committed to the graphic arts as to criticism and literature. Bruce Rogers was employed as designer with an open-ended mandate to respect the beauties of type, format, and paper. The magazine held to a somewhat conservative but quite elegant traditional design. Reproductions were carefully selected for works that could be predictably captured by available processes and Thayer made those decisions. Early in the publication's new life he elected not to reproduce ". . . anything that had been reproduced before in America." [93] *The Dial*'s internationalism was in opposition to the main body of early twentieth century American criticism. It was a magazine for writers and artists which paid for all pieces and reproductions. Its circulation went up to 18,000 during the first four years. The deficit often went as high as $50,000 a year during that period. Circulation eventually reached its "natural" level between 2,000 and 4,000 during the last five years." [94]

In examining the early issues of *The Dial* as published by Thayer and Watson, one finds it to be a magazine of criticism, with a heavy commitment to literature, theatre, music, and modern art commentary and with only a lesser amount of space for fiction and poetry. Such critics as W. B. Yeats, Romain Rolland, Amy Lowell, D. H. Lawrence, Marcel Proust, Bertrand Russell, Jean Cocteau, Benedetto Croce, Kenneth Burke, John Dos Passos, Jean Giradoux, Wyndham Lewis, Maxwell Bodenheim, George Santayana, and Arthur Schnitzler are joined by such reviewers and creative writers as Babette Deutsch, Slater Brown, Sherwood Anderson, Vachel Lindsay, Hart Crane, Malcolm Cowley, Conrad Aiken, John Dos Passos, Padraic Colum, Amy Lowell, and E. E. Cummings. At the same time the reproductions of art works included examples by Cezanne, Demuth, Burchfield, Marin, Pascin, Redon and Gaston Lachaise, Stuart Davis, William Gropper, Derain, Lipchitz, Arthur B. Davies, Gauguin, Vlaminck and van Gogh, Flannagan, Zorach, Storrs, Nadelman, O'Keeffe, Weber, Picasso and Zadkine. Such men as Picasso and Lachaise tend to dominate the pages.

"Modern Forms," a new department, carried the subtitle "This department of *The Dial* is devoted to exposition and consideration of the less traditional types of Art." The guide to "Modern Forms"—Henry McBride wrote: ". . . a first rate exhibition by a serious artist, Gaston Lachaise, was given in the Bourgeois Galleries in February and appeared to escape attention. Not even Chicago could have been more obtuse to a subtle and original art than was New York." [95] The February issue of *The Dial* had featured an important essay on Lachaise' art by E. E. Cummings. Lachaise was indeed the sculptor of *The Dial* and he occupied a position of special importance in the minds of the shapers of its editorial policies.

Thayer and Watson drew to themselves a number of equally broad and dedicated editorial colleagues, including Gilbert Seldes, associate and managing editor, 1920–23, Alyse Gregory, managing editor, 1924–25, Marianne Moore (Fig. 29), acting editor and later editor, 1926–29. These editorial leaders utilized regular critics for theatre—Gilbert Seldes; modern art—Henry McBride; music—Paul Rosenfeld. At different points these writers were complemented by Kenneth Burke, Clive Bell, Roger Fry, and even George Santayana.

The Dial operated for nine and one-half years through the July 1929 number. It became an influential voice for international standards in literature and the plastic arts. Ezra Pound's *Hugh Selwyn Mauberly* had its first publication in the September 1920 number. The November 1922 issue provided the first printing of *The Waste Land* by T. S. Eliot. Thomas Mann's *Death in Venice* was one of the masterpieces of 1924's record. Such distinguished international figures (nowadays) as Yeats, Valery, D. H. Lawrence, Ford Madox Ford, and William Carlos Williams were repeatedly given space in the magazine. European "Letters" on literary and sometimes related subjects were printed recurrently from Germany (Thomas Mann), Paris (Ezra Pound), London (T. S. Eliot), Italy (Rafaello Piccoli), Vienna (Ortega y Gasset), Dublin (Hugo von Hofmannstahl), and Russia (Maxim Gorki). This wide ranging and patently prescient editorial achievement came about as the result of the dedication and seriousness of the owners and their chosen editorial assistants.

The print-oriented reader is said to have found the literary-critical content easier to accept than he did the graphics and reproductions of paintings and sculpture. The French masters of modernism highlighted by the magazine were Picasso, Matisse, Bonnard, and Derain. Maillol and Lehmbruck were featured sculptors. Such comparatively little-known artists at that time as Klimt, Munch, Kokoschka, Barlach, Schiele, and Delaunay were given prominent placement after Thayer's stay in Europe. Marin, Demuth, and Lachaise were his primary American enthusiasms, but lesser figures received attention from time to time.

Thayer's imagination was taken by the practice in the German publishing firms of producing facsimile reproductions of nineteenth-century masters' work of the highest quality. He resolved to make such a portfolio, selecting the artists himself in order to show America the variety of exciting work being done in Europe and America in the plastic arts. He conceived of buying the art so that a concurrent exhibition of it could elicit comparisons in press reviews. The project drew on and cost considerably more than was originally planned, but the works were verified by the printers for color and quality. All of the selections turned out to be figurative and no cubist material found its way into the portfolio. Picasso (Blue and Rose periods), Segonzac, Laurencin, as well as Matisse and Bonnard were selected. Marin, Demuth, Lachaise, Pascin, Maillol, and Mestrovic were included. (Lachaise' *Mountain* had two views.) The collection was shown first at the Montross Gallery in New York City, later at the Worcester Art Museum, and finally at Smith College. The portfolios were received with critical approval but sales were slow and eventually the price was reduced from $60 and the edition of 400 copies for sale was sold out. Thayer's commitment to contemporary art was consistent with his efforts.

Gaston Lachaise enjoyed twenty-three full page reproductions, four full essays and four more partial essays as well as a number of complimentary mentions in eighteen separate issues over its 115-month life. The essays were written by E. E. Cummings (February 1920), Paul Rosenfeld (September 1926), Thomas Craven (June 1923), and Henry McBride on numerous occasions, including August 1920, June 1927, and March 1928. It is important to realize that the initial issue of the new management utilized the artist's bas relief *Dusk* as its frontispiece. Drawings, figure sculptures, nonportrait busts made up the major part of the black and white reproductions of Lachaise' art in *The Dial*. The modeled portraits of E. E. Cummings (Fig. 28), Scofield Thayer, Dr. James Sibley Watson, Jr. (Fig. 30), and Henry McBride, as published in the journal, gave evidence of a high level of support by the magazine's management. Hildegarde Watson, the publisher's wife, posed for a full-length figure. Marianne Moore, editor, and Gilbert Seldes, managing editor (and eventually his wife and both children), were sculptured by Lachaise. Moving outside the magazine itself to important figures in the art community who were, in turn, celebrated by *The Dial*, one must mention portraits of Marin, Van Vechten, O'Keeffe, Stieglitz, Mrs. Bertram Hartmann (published in the January 1924 number), Antoinette Kraushaar, the author M. R. Werner, and Juliana Force of the Whitney Museum, among many others.

New York Galleries

When he first made the rounds of the New York galleries in 1916 or 1917 with the intent of arranging a one-man show of his work, Lachaise had set Alfred Stieglitz apart as an exhibitor of unusual importance. He had never spoken to Stieglitz until he asked the awkward question and received the elder man's tart rejoinder referred to earlier. In the succeeding years the two men came to know each other, and both Stieglitz and his wife, Georgia O'Keeffe, posed for portrait busts. An exchange of letters over the period of thirty-two months directly prior to the stock market crash may serve to show the climate of support and warmth as well as the desperate frustration which Lachaise felt in ". . . doing everything he could do to keep my boat from sinking . . ." as he said to Marianne Moore. Moore herself spoke of Lachaise' ". . . character wrought by adversity and . . . a dissent to the world of compromise." She perceived what she termed his "congenital inescape from that adversity." [96]

December 5, 1926. Lachaise to Stieglitz: "I have a life size marble that you saw the plaster of last year. If you feel the possibility of a small exhibition I would like to have you to see these new things. . . ."

December 7, 1926. Stieglitz to Lachaise: ". . . Marin til the 15. Then O'Keeffe January 17 and run through February. March will be free. In case of sales we would not accept commissions.[97] It is as our guest that we want you here and a most welcome one you would be."

The exhibition at The Intimate Gallery was held in 1927. A three panel, double-fold checklist was prepared from 8¼ by 10 inch stock. The cover panel announced "Gaston Lachaise Sculptures" at The Intimate Gallery: Room 303, The Anderson Galleries Building, 489 Park Avenue, New York, from March 7 to April 3, 1927. Twenty sculptures were listed on the third panel: eight statuettes, six portraits, two seagulls, *The Mountain* (Fig. 55), a mask, a torso, and a marble relief. Thirteen of the works were listed as on loan to the exhibition, of which three were owned by Mme. Lachaise.

The show was well received and there were sales. In addition Stieglitz arranged meetings for portraits and other commissions. Lachaise' letters in May speak of Mrs. Liebmann's project, in June they treat of Goodwin, Gorham, and Biddle, and in September he announced: "Good news—Mr. Goodwin is very pleased with the plaster model just completed of the half life-size figure. . . . The 'impulse' I received from you this winter is carrying through." A warm letter from the Stieglitzes dated May 2, 1927, is of particular interest:

My dear Lachaise: I have been thinking a great deal about my portrait. And the more I think of what you have done the better I like it. It's a devilishly difficult thing for even one as *free* as myself to get away from the stupid "likeness" habit—it is ever getting in the way—*at first*. Gradually it disappears entirely and one is free to really *see* what is before one. Then the true contact is completely established—I want you to know that I feel really delighted to know the Portrait will soon exist in its final state. I appreciate what a tough job you had—and more than appreciate your appreciation of me—I think you know my feelings about (you) as a person—as a worker—really all one. May be some day I'll get to photographing again and then I can more clearly show you what I see—feel. Our greetings to you and the Madam—Stieglitz.

Georgia saw your bronze head at the Lewisohn's today—It looked very beautiful. She tells me to tell you.

Lachaise wrote to Stieglitz on July 7, 1927, to Lake George where he habitually summered:

Thank you for the two photographs. I am very happy to have them. I shall have to part with them for the time to send them to my wife (in Maine). I have the bronze portrait of you in the studio. The casting in bronze have done great thing for it and make it possible to work further on it. This is a great time for me. . . .

Despite the sense of friendship and mutual respect which is carried in these exchanges, Lachaise' financial problems were dreadfully real and disturbing. During the Autumn of 1927 he was invited to show with Joseph Brummer at his Fifty-seventh Street Gallery. It was an unspoken understanding that Lachaise could not expect to become a member of the inner circle of The Intimate Gallery despite his relationship with Stieglitz as a favored guest. Lachaise arranged to show with Brummer in late February–March of the following year. Twenty-eight sculptures were shown including nine portraits; ten female figures—standing, dancing, walking, seated, reclining, and in a number of acrobatic postures. The portraits included Isabel, Marin, Cummings, Henry Straiter (sic), Dr. L. Pierce Clark, Henry McBride, Dr. James M. Murphy, Helen Teschner Tas, and the first showing of the bust of Alfred Stieglitz.[98]

Madame Lachaise always spoke of the Brummer exhibition as Lachaise' finest one-man show in a commercial gallery. It afforded the first public exhibition of the bronze *Standing Woman*, (*Elevation*), 1912–27, the first viewing of the *Floating Woman*, 1927, as well as a number of his new fragment sculptures. McBride wrote ecstatically of the show in both *The Dial* and the catalog of the exhibition, saying of Lachaise' career:

The one artist among us whose visions towered mountingly in sizes comparable with our architecture was the artist New York chose to ignore. . . . I expect her (New York) now to come around to the Lachaise "Woman." I was immensely surprised when calling on the sculptor . . . to find this goddess that I have been writing about, there, and in the bronze, the shiny surfaces of which are prodigiously becoming to her. If possible she is more amazing and satisfactory than ever. In my mind's eye I already have visions of her, and the stir she will make, in the Musée du Luxembourg. . . .[99]

Writing in *Creative Art* for August 1928, E. E. Cummings said:

. . . to summarize Lachaise's achievement . . . is primarily to collide with a solitude unique, firm, sudden, homogeneous. The solitude called sculpture, of Lachaise, does not date; never describes; cannot pretend. Once within its clutch, we everywhere encounter nothing archaic, nothing modern, nothing unexperienced—everywhere we find ourselves conjugated by a mind which feels freely. . . . Take, for example . . . a vitality so unmitigated as to become invisible, an almost impertinent fulfillment, supreme luxury of fruition. Pass to these five or six figures, not motion because movement, antithesis of imitation, neither adjectival nor adverbial, unmodifying, actual, not real, distinct, sufficient, reflexive—the one self reddish golden, the other self black; this tumbles, that sprints; another (asquirm, fused) lustily upspouts, innumerably answering the spiral question of mortality. Contrast with a focused and brutal and centrifugal sexually idiom, sprawled yet flying, one gradual collocation of breasts and thighs, one single effortless glide of volume or faultlessly promulgating structure. . . .[100]

During the latter part of 1927 and the first few months of 1928 Lachaise returned borrowed moneys to Stieglitz, received sums in payment for old transactions as well as new ones, and occasionally asked for prompter payment. On October 11, 1928, Stieglitz wrote:

My dear Lachaise: While lying in bed for these weeks and ordered not to think—much passed thru my mind without "thinking." I am enclosing your check for $243.50 ($250 minus costs of wiring you moneys) which means you will have received $1000 for your statuette *without* any commissions off—I don't like the idea of "commission" for The Room. It is really *against* all I feel.

The Room doesn't *need* the cash and you certainly do—that is you can use it—we "can't." So please don't say thank you nor try to argue with me.

I'm doing the *only* thing to be true to *all* of us—plus something beyond that. Heaven knows what it can be called—or even what it is.

I hope you are at work and that the Iselins realize that given half a chance you do know how to make good on time! Then . . . that work is in sight—My (our) cordial greetings to you and the Madam— ever your old Stieglitz.

Toward the end of the year Lachaise thanked Stieglitz for yet another loan before writing of the Stieglitz bust: "I do not think it can be see; until all by itself in the center of a room on a slender pedestal. . . ." In December a repayment check was returned to Stieglitz "short of funds." In the first week of 1929, Lachaise wrote, "Sorry that I can't send you a new check just now . . . early as I can arrange it. . . ." and continued:

I would have come to see as you suggested through the phone but I find it for me at the present and under the general pressure that I am facing, not to take a chance with my ugly temper—and not to bear with it on my friends.

I must say that the day I called you on the phone I obeyed to a impulse to be nasty which developed during my walk back downtown with the gull under my hand—my wife pointed to the nasty little boy way of me when I told her the story. I am always sorry for my bad impulse. Sincerely yours, Lachaise.

May 3, 1928. My dear Lachaise: Pardon my not sending you this sooner. It was impossible. As you know I'm alone—I find I have given you $1000 since November last. And I have as collateral the little bronze torso—the mask—the torso in alabaster and the polished brass figure. Now to clean up this matter I suggest the following: I shall give you $200 for the small bronze torso—$325 for the polished brass figure (old one)—$325 for the marble torso. That makes $850 for these three pieces. That means you still owe me $150. You need not worry about that. Sometime that can be cleaned up. The mask is yours. Should some one want the marble (alabaster/torso) whatever it may bring over $325 will be divided in equal parts between you and The Room.

I want this matter cleared up not only for your sake but for my own. I dislike ragged edges. I hope all this will satisfy you. If not just be frank. As you know I am doing all this for you at your own request. I wish I were in a position to really put you on your feet. Greetings, Stieglitz.

May 13, 1929. Dear Lachaise, we have to vacate Room 303 and I beg of you to remove within 10 days the 2 small bronzes and the 2 small alabaster pieces which you left in The Room on your own responsibility. p.s. The four pieces I am asking you to remove, I did not ask for as a collateral nor have I ever asked you or another artist for collateral or a receipt nor has any other artist asked me for a receipt.

May 16, 1929. My dear Lachaise, I regret exceedingly what occurred last Monday afternoon. More than I can say. Since the happening I have thought and thought about the ghastly situation which I feel you have created and possibly I have too in my real innocence in trying to protect you from what I take the liberty to call yourself. I see only one way to bring this matter to a close and I refuse any further discussion.

Since November 7, 1928, you received from me $1000. You came to me the very day I returned from Lake George and pleaded with me to let you have $200, saying that you were in desperate circumstances and that your wife was sick in Maine and you wished to spare her. I ill, just out of bed with heart trouble, not wishing to excite myself, had no alternative, even though I was in no position to meet your wishes, but to give you the $200. A few days later you

came again in despair and asked for $500, more. And again I gave
you this money. Again I had no choice because of my feelings for
you and for your wife, knowing your desperate position. Not much
after, you came and begged me to cash a check for $200, for you,
saying that in two weeks you expected money and so, although fearing that the check would not be met when deposited, I wished to
show you my complete confidence in you, so you received the $200.
And when the check was eventually deposited it came back marked
"no funds." And you never said a word. Nor did I say anything. In
all this I acted as if I were a man of means which you know I am
not.

Eventually you came and asked for another $100. This after you
had one morning insulted me. . . . Of your own volition, I not suggesting it, you brought to The Room, as collateral, a dark bronze
torso . . . a highly polished brass . . . statuette, 1919 . . . torso in
alabaster . . . a mask. . . .

To my amazement a couple of weeks ago you appear out of a clear
sky and come to me and ask for a receipt for these four pieces. I was
dumfounded at the request. I told you that such a request had never
been made by anyone from me. . . . But I met your wish. . . .

Translated into plain English, that instead of $850, you were receiv-
ing $1000 for what I considered liberally paid for at $850. . . .

You told me that you *must* turn your things into cash. That your
situation was desperate. You and Mrs. Lachaise gave me the figures,
they ranged from $600 . . . to $800, and the bas-relief $1000. Sev-
eral people inquired the cost of some of the pieces and when I gave
them your figures they laughed and said that there were similar
pieces at Kraushaar's at much lower figures. I told them how that
came about and explained your situation. You know that your situation with virtually all your so-called clients was a rather messy one.
I tried to make them understand how as a "business man" you were
your own worst enemy as many artists are. . . .

The three pieces which I had accepted as payment for the $1000
given you since November 1, 1928, I return to you. The $1000 you
may keep . . . I am satisfied to pay for the lesson and hope you are
satisfied with your bonus. This ends the matter. . . .

Will you please call for, or have called for within ten days, the mask,
and the three other pieces which again belong to you. We have to
vacate the Room so I would consider it a special favor if you did
this as soon as possible. All this, I think, brings our relationship into
clarity. At least I hope so.

Please do not forget that your four pieces are here at your own risk.
Sincerely, Stieglitz.

Undated letter on Brevoort stationary: Dear Mr. Stieglitz, I have
read several times and thought over your letter of May 16.

If you feel that in returning to me the walking figure, 1919, the alabaster torso (slender type) the bronze torso, and the mask in alabaster you still get the full value of your money in keeping the bronze figure "La Montagne," the alabaster torso, and the small nickel figure, I shall be satisfied.

But I cannot from you accept either a bonus or that as you say you shall "pay for your lesson."

In such a case I would propose that I may buy bac from you as early as possible the several sculptures mentioned above.

May I take the opportunity of this letter to assure you of my profound gratitude for what you have done for me so generously and so courageously, and May I say that my demands for a written statement of your verbal propositions was but to conform to the advice which you have repeatedly given to me, to have a written understanding done even with my best friend. Sincerely yours, Gaston Lachaise.

1 June 1929. Alfred Stieglitz to Gaston Lachaise: First of all won't you please do me the favor to get your four bits of sculpture belonging to you out of the Room.

I have your letter of the 26th. All I have to say is that I am perfectly satisfied to have you realize that I have given you $2200 for La Montagne, the alabaster torso (2 years ago) and the nickel figure and consider the whole matter closed.

I wish you to know that my admiration for much of your work is as great as ever and that as an individual I esteem you but have come to the realisation that for some reason or other your way and my way of doing things do not seem to come together any more. This is probably my fault as much as yours. . . . Alfred Stieglitz.

Patrons and Commissions

During 1927 Lachaise worked on a sculptural portrait of Gregory Slader, a friend of the architect Phillip Goodwin. It was first executed in a forty-two-inch marble in 1927 and carried further in 1928 into a life-size bronze now in the Philadelphia Museum. Titled *Figure of a Nude Athlete*, the bronze measured seventy-six inches in height and might have been expected to have been an important work in Lachaise' career, but the artist didn't respond to it as creative work of his but saw it as a "bread earning task." "The bottom of it is that I do not know and love the male figure as I do the woman." [101] Also in 1928, working with the architectural firm of Mellor, Meigs and Howe, Lachaise was commissioned to do a sculpture of a spread-winged sea gull for the U.S. Coast Guard Memorial sculpture for Arlington Cemetery, in Virginia. Letters in the correspondence with Isabel reflect his concern for the work and his preparations for trips to Philadelphia or Washington in connection with the commission.

During the late twenties Phillip Goodwin saw Lachaise a great deal, and commissioned a number of works. Goodwin felt that the *Man* of 1930–34 was an outgrowth of his commissions of the athlete in marble and the later life-sized figure. In addition, Goodwin commissioned a *Swan Fountain* in 1931, the peacock sculptures for the Deering Estate, two decorative squirrel reliefs for his own home on Long Island, and he bought a Marin portrait bust to give to the Wadsworth Atheneum (Hartford). Goodwin admired Lachaise' work but he felt no closeness to him as a man—"there was never any personal relationship." [102] Goodwin also expressed the feeling that "Lachaise was a very demanding fellow and always in need of money." A sketch book given by Lachaise to Goodwin of studies made during July and August 1927 records forty-one sittings, thirty-seven of which were two hours in duration with two each longer and shorter in duration.

In his private work Lachaise was engaged in a modest scale on his fragment sculptures (Figs. 73–85)—torsos which evolved through the Ogunquit and Classic style to the more expressionistic development of his ideas in shell forms. This is the year of *Burlesque* (Fig. 19) and the beginnings of experiments which come to fruition in the thirties giving birth to more advanced developments which were left incomplete at the end.

The Dial magazine sadly discontinued publication after the July 1929 issue. Two years before, in September 1927, a group of Harvard undergraduates under the leadership of Lincoln Kirstein (A.B., 1929, A.M., 1930) began a publication called *Harvard Miscellany*, with Kirstein as editor and R. P. Blackmur and A. Hyatt Mayor as associate editors. The magazine was patterned after *The Dial* in its respect for criticism and reviews with an emphasis on the great figures in Harvard's recent literary past. By the Fall of 1930 the magazine had changed its name to *Hound and Horn* and moved its editorial offices to New York City. Set in a handsome ten- by six-inch format, running approximately 150 pages a quarterly issue, with between 2,500 and 3,000 in circulation, the well-presented journal continued the nascent doctrine of formalist criticism which lay at the base of *The Dial,* under the editorial direction of Allen Tate, Yvor Winters, and R. P. Blackmur.

In addition to his interest in literature and criticism Kirstein was a founder in 1927 of the Harvard Society for Modern Art, which offered exhibitions at Harvard in the late twenties. Edward M. M. Warburg (B.S., 1930) provided the monetary support for the Society and Kirstein had a free hand in the aesthetic programming. They borrowed works from dealers and collectors and provided exhibitions in Cambridge through 1930. Kirstein began his correspondence with Lachaise at that time, aware of the artist through *The Dial* and his New York exhibitions, he invited the sculptor to participate in exhibitions offered by the Harvard Society. A letter from Lachaise to Kirstein, dated April 1, 1929, thanked him for copies of the announcement-catalog of the exhibition and for copies of the clipping, adding, "Your statement about my work in the catalog pleased me."

Kirstein was the son of Louis Edward Kirstein, a successful merchant and vice president of the Filene Company, and Rose Stein of the Rochester family. He was the second of three children and had sufficient money as an undergraduate, twenty years old, to found the magazine. He associated himself with a brilliant assortment of literary and art-oriented people, including Edward M. M. Warburg, of New York. Through Kirstein, Warburg became deeply committed to the Society, to collecting, and within a short time to Lachaise, his art and his financial problems.

Man, the eight-foot final statement of Lachaise on the male figure, was completed in plaster in 1930 and exhibited at the newly opened Museum of Modern Art, New York, 730 Fifth Avenue, Manhattan, under the guidance of Alfred H. Barr, Jr. Established with Rockefeller backing, the Museum of Modern Art began with an awareness of Gaston Lachaise, and under the persuasive guidance of Lincoln Kirstein and two men who would soon be trustees of that institution— Edward M. M. Warburg and Nelson Rockefeller—came to know and admire the work and the artist in some depth.

Lachaise kept moving, restlessly developing new work, finishing older pieces, reconsidering works in progress. It was in 1931 that he brought two emphatic sculptures begun in 1928 to completion: *Striding Woman* (Fig. 16) and *Reclining Woman* (Fig. 50), both of which were shown in plaster in the 1935 retrospective at the Museum of Modern Art. These expressionist figures relate to the *Heroic Woman* but actually go beyond it, suggesting life-scaled works for the future, anticipating suggestions of movement and energy unparalleled in Lachaise' art.

While he was experimenting at his own art, Lachaise continued his commercial exercises on a number of lines. Phillip Goodwin commissioned a *Swan Fountain* which was placed in Brook Green Gardens, S. Carolina, and Lachaise became deeply involved in it. At the same time, he was working on a bust of the author Carl Van Vechten, who had been urged by Gilbert Seldes to make the commission. The Van Vechten bust was a great critical success and brought attention to both the artist and subject.

Seldes was at one of his most flush periods with his translation and staging of *Lysistrata* running on Broadway. He commissioned Lachaise to do a bust of his son, Timothy, and then followed with his wife, his daughter, and himself in his efforts to help Lachaise' financial situation.

Early in the thirties Lachaise was involved with plans for the Chicago World's Fair. The contract was eventually signed and the artist undertook a twenty-foot relief sculpture for the Electricity Building titled *The Conquest of Time and Space*. The dominant element in the composition is a male figure. Negative and positive electrical poles at the bottom of the composition are shown with humanity marching toward them. Above and behind the male figure, depictions of generators, searchlights, telescopes, and telephone and telegraph wires symbolize communications. The figure—"Human Genius"— wears headphones and between his widespread hands is the diagram of radiography. The title of the piece was set out in bold relief at the upper margin of the twenty-foot panel with its two side panels. The work was installed for the first year of the fair, 1932, painted in polychrome, and it was stripped of its color for the second year and utilized as a white relief.

It was in 1931 that Gilbert Seldes did his *Profile* of Gaston Lachaise, "Hewer of Stone," for the *New Yorker* magazine. Lachaise apparently sat down in his Brevoort Hotel room with its bare bulb and penned in longhand a thirty-five page holographic autobiography which began with his birth and ventured through childhood experiences, the Beaux-Arts, meeting Isabel, up to the Brummer Gallery show of 1928. One of the fascinating anecdotes of Seldes' *Profile* had to do with a story also told by Mme. Lachaise, Nakian, and others having to do with A. Stirling Calder, serving as a juror:

. . . a group of artists more or less associated with the academies had decided to be liberal and had formed an exhibition to which they invited experimental sculptors to submit their most characteristic work. Lachaise sent in seven pieces, some in bronze and the others in plaster. As he was working in the exhibition room he noticed one of the judges—an artist himself—moving Lachaise's cast from one obscure corner to another, with an expression of considerable pain, as if he wished the walls would open and swallow up these unusual sculptures. Presently he went into another room and after a few moments a message was brought to Lachaise that one of his casts had been broken. Lachaise hurried back to collect the fragments, and while he was gathering them up, a man came over and told him that a second cast had been smashed. Both had fallen from the hands of the same judge, both by accident—the kind of accident which comes of suppressed desires. To guard his property Lachaise removed the rest of his casts. When he began to work on one of the broken ones, the figure of a woman lying on a couch, he found himself unwilling to repeat what he had done; the figure took on more ample proportions, and slowly freed itself from the background, until after months of labor it became the "Floating Figure," . . . a miracle of composition in spheres and curves to those for whom sculpture is an art and not a report. . . .[103]

Seldes' article was a prestigious event for Lachaise. Occurring at a low time in economic affairs, it nonetheless set him in a class totally apart from any other sculptor of his time. The *New Yorker* profile was a part of the fashion media and it was attended to much more closely than the more serious articles of greater intellectual merit from *The Dial*. Seldes, an ex-*Dial* editor and devoted patron of the artist, utilized the holographic autobiography in telling the story of Lachaise' life in art, continuing,

Lachaise has had to skip entirely that stage in an artist's work between obscurity and greatness, the stage of publicized success out of which many artists never move, bogged in the luxuriant and rather pleasant swamp of social esteem and easy money. On the other hand, every piece of sculpture which he has made in stone or metal in the last fifteen years has been bought, and the only things left in his studio are plasters which have not yet been cast or cut. It is remarkable also that his chief patrons stand at the two extremes: conservative collectors and museums on one side, and what might be called the *Dial* group on the other, so that he is represented in the collections of Adolph Lewisohn and Alfred Stieglitz simultaneously, and has done a statuette for Mrs. John D. Rockefeller, Jr., and a head of E E Cummings, and has been praised by Royal Cortissoz and Paul Strand, and appears in the American Telephone and Telegraph Building and in Gallatin's Gallery of Living Art.[104]

Seldes' piece was a richly deserved eulogy which joined to many lesser spreads in *Vanity Fair, Parnassus, Art News, Magazine of Art, Creative Art,* and other leading magazines of taste and merit. Lincoln Kirstein's own *Hound and Horn* published the commentary of A. Hyatt Mayor on Gaston Lachaise in the third quarter of 1932, where he said: ". . . whatever it was that endowed him with this humility, it thereby enabled him to become the finest portrait sculptor now living. . . . The concentration of individual life in Lachaise's heads often reminds one of Houdon, since both of them dramatize a character in action. Yet unlike Houdon, who builds up his heads by pellets applied to a core, Lachaise is a true sculptor, a stonecutter who chisels a block to uncover the head inside, so that the result retains something of the original block's massiveness. . . . Lachaise is the only sculptor in this country who handles the medium with the assurance of a master experienced in all its possibilities, and too reverent to force them."

Lachaise was enjoying a ground swell of critical success, a visibility which might be compared to present day jet-setters. Discussions were initiated with the Museum of Modern Art concerning an exhibition. He was a candidate for a major commission for Rockefeller Center, then under construction. Eventually the Rockefeller Center commission came while the Museum of Modern Art project continued to seem far off at the end of a long series of tantalizing possibilities. In a letter to Isabel Lachaise wrote: "Warburg said the situation at the Museum was that all the young people like you, but the old ones say why that man with his fat women. Also trustees have husbands and wives who do not like Lachaise. Others say Lachaise is a very disagreeable man, you will be involved in all sorts of trouble. I am called a disagreeable man unjustly sometimes, justly more or less sometime. Many people use that against me to favor their interest." [105]

Eventually the Rockefeller contract was let, and Lachaise was to do a series of four panels in limestone on the Sixth Avenue face of the R.C.A. Building, between thirty and fifty feet above the street. The allegorical fashion of that day called for a theme—"The Conquest of Space," "The Spirit of Progress," "Gifts of Earth to Mankind," and "Genius Seizing the Light of the Sun." Lachaise did sketches and models and adjusted his rather world's fairish designs to the judgment of the architects' and owners' committee. Final work was executed in place, on a scaffold high above Sixth Avenue with the then present elevated trains crashing by in their swift and noisy fashion.

Lincoln Kirstein (Fig. 40) engaged Lachaise to make a portrait bust of him in 1932, while the big commissions were in stages of negotiation and while Lachaise' own work on the *Heroic Woman,* the new torsos, and other portraits was developing. The Kirstein head was not entirely successful from the subject's point of view but it has been widely praised elsewhere, "as insecure, sensitive, highly geared—full of catalytic energy." [106] No sooner had this piece been finished than Kirstein sat for Lachaise as he began a nude portrait of the young intellectual in the manner of an Egyptian king. Warburg "saw nothing odd in the nude Kirstein sculpture—everything was a formal relationship to Lachaise."

A. E. Gallatin, the author of the 1924 monograph on Lachaise, brought George L. K. Morris, the painter, to Lachaise' studio and suggested that Morris (Fig. 42) give Lachaise some work. The work began with the bust and progressed over a period of time to the nude figure with tennis racket (Fig. 45) and finally in 1934 to the *Montagne Heroique* (Fig. 56). Morris said of Lachaise:

He was a lovable person . . . like a kid. . . . his most distinctive characteristic was that there was no "fakery"—nothing but genuineness —about Lachaise. . . . Everything that Lachaise said was interesting, bearing out the fact that his thoughts were carefully considered and that he never talked just to talk. . . . Lachaise had a good mind but it was warped by the persecution idea and by the money disease . . . that if he inherited several millions that he would have continued to touch people.[107]

Kirstein brought Warburg to the studio a number of times during the very early 1930s. It is clear in retrospect that Warburg became one of Lachaise' most important patrons and one of the few able to follow the artist's most expansive and experimental developments. His gifts of the *Standing Figure* and the *Torso* (Fig. 84) in stone to Smith College and his purchases for his own collection of *The Knees* (Fig. 85), the *Torso of the Heroic Woman,* the *Breasts* of 1933 (Fig. 83), and the sole life-time cast of *The Dynamo Mother* (Fig. 82), attest to that vision and courage. Lachaise finally agreed to make a Warburg portrait and executed it in a precious alabaster, after developing a satisfactory likeness in plasticene. "It is a great thing—He is very enthusiasm for it—I do like Warburg very much.[108] Warburg showed great concern for Lachaise' human frailty in handling money as indicated in a Gaston Lachaise letter to Isabel:

(Warburg) . . . told me he had arranged his expenses in a budged and that he was putting $5,000 for me for the course of next year. He told me "I would give you a check to open a bank account but I know that you would have nothing left in two months and I doubt that you would be secure for even part of a year. I want to know how I can make you free and calm. The studio of Manship (on Washington Mews is for rent but they want a full year—$1,500)." He told me that he would guarantee that sum. . . .[109]

Lachaise wrote to Isabel in early 1933, "Kirstein has spoken at the Museum (of Modern Art) for a one-man show— wanted it this year. But that is to be given to Maurice Sterne, to please Lewisohn whose collection they hope to inherit. They are considering a date for me next Spring."[110] In another note dated June 30, 1933, to his stepson Edward Nagle, Lachaise added: "The Modern Museum show is still undecided as date at least Warburg working very devotedly for it say that they may have to wait a year to have it as perfect as they want it. Mr. Goodyear will be out of the Museum then and they expect to have more freedom then. Barr, the director (and Nelson Rockefeller), is all for it. . . ."

Lachaise received a second commission from Rockefeller Center in 1934. In this assignment he was allotted two reliefs on the rear or east side of the International Building which fronts at 630 Fifth Avenue. Directly cut in limestone, on the spot, the site has greater visibility in location and an improved angle of vision for the passerby. In the right element two male figures at ground level are dismantling a Greek column with what appear to be steel tools. The left figure is in profile, facing the masked figure on the right, also in profile. In the element on the left one finds two male figures riding upward on a girder, lifted presumably by a crane, in the building of a new city. The figures are lightly skirted male nudes. This celebration of the workers who built the Center, tearing down preexisting buildings and raising the brave new dream city, was arrived at as a theme with the architects.[111] In his letters Lachaise confesses he is using models for these figures: "I am having a debauch of work. I am undressing all my male friends. Nison (sic) not so good—rather disappointing, soft and weak; Geegee very much to the point, a sort of dwarf type of the real strong fellow needed for this work. Kirstein will come next week. I am using the advantage of models as a starting base for this work."[112]

A number of important works were brought to completion in 1934. They serve to demonstrate the continued variety and vitality of the artist even under the pressures of the Rockefeller Center commissions, the negotiations with the Samuels Memorial Committee in Philadelphia, and his persistent money worries. A medical doctor engaged Lachaise to do a bust of his lady friend, a Mrs. Morgan, and Lachaise began in his normal fashion. Soon, at his suggestion, Mrs. Morgan had agreed that it should be a nude quarter figure, then half-figure and eventually it was to become a full nude figure (Fig. 43). In a letter of November 29, 1934, Lachaise reported to Isabel, whom he sometimes called Belle:

I have the Mountain for Morris ready to mold in cement and I have finished molding the bas relief begun in Georgetown and nearly finished Mrs. Morgan which is now just down to the lower belly. She came four hours last week. Eventually they want a full figure. . . .

Lachaise had indeed taken on the task of the large mountain for George L. K. Morris, after visiting the artist's Lenox, Massachusetts, estate and agreeing on its site in a pine forest. During the same months the artist was diligently developing his last version of the *Love* theme from his second Bourgeois show—a standing male figure holding his mate in his arms while they kiss. Closely related to Indian temple sculpture, the twenty-six-inch piece is nonetheless a development from the classical beginnings of Lachaise' art and indicative of the path he might have traveled in his full scale works had he sufficient life and time. The final and smallest adventure of the period was a less than twenty-inch *Acrobat Woman* (Fig. 72), closely related to the 1929 sculpture of the same name. Lachaise' faith in these works is evidenced in that both were included in the Museum of Modern Art Retrospective; both were reproduced on the same page of the exhibition's catalog. This work suggested a powerful new generalization of forms which carried Lachaise' art into entirely new territory. As the artist said to a reporter, subsequently reported in *Art Digest:*

I am constantly evolving, changing, growing. Sometime, years ago, I used to think maybe I was crazy because other people did. It takes much belief in your work to last ten years. But they have accepted my mode of expression and now when I make a work there is renewed hostility. I am not a maniac, I simply can't stand still, doing the same statue time and time again as some painters who are content to go to sleep. . . .[113]

Lachaise often expressed his admiration for his wife to others, not only in publications like the *Creative Art* piece or in the holographic autobiography. Every one of his friends and associates knew of his devotion. Many felt that his

Isabel

respect and gratitude was overdone, that it might indeed be a flaw in his nature. Many speakers suggested that Madame Lachaise was extravagant and that her expensive tastes kept him unnecessarily in difficult circumstances.

On one occasion Lachaise admitted to Allys and Marie, his mother, when they were visiting in Georgetown, "We need 20,000 to 30,000 a year." "Why?" asked his mother, "Why not cut your costs?" Mme. Lachaise replied "Why he's young, he can work." [114] Allys herself mentioned Lachaise having a studio at Washington Mews, with an apartment on top, while Mme. Lachaise stayed at One Fifth Avenue in a suite with a living room, bedroom, bath, and Lachaise had still another place at the Brevoort. [115]

He said, as reported in Arts Digest, February 1, 1935: "You may say that the model (of *The Mountain*) is my wife. It is a large, generous figure of great placidity, great tranquility. Whatever I have of tranquility I get from my wife. . . . What I am aiming to express is the glorification of the human being, of the human body, of the human spirit with all that there is of daring, magnificence. . . ." [116]

Hundreds of letters from Lachaise to Isabel from wherever he was, written whenever they were separated, demonstrate his constant concern for her well being, thought about her comfort, her flowers, cold cream, tea, the maid, and sending money. He always expressed his love and concern in a touching fashion. Oftentimes he would include a drawing, perhaps of a standing figure with a caption, "The best of ALL Me all Over you IN and Out." [117] Or a tiny view of her bedroom with a man and woman lying side by side. In one letter a picture of Isabel in bed with a cat at the foot of the bed, she enjoying a breakfast tray with captions: "blue kimona I hope." "Pink one is coming." Pointing to the teacup: "Koefler's best," and "cream."

A few letters from the final years give one a sense of the tensions which Isabel, Gaston, and her son Edward suffered. [118]

In the first few years of the 1930s it was not unusual for families of three and four persons to subsist on between $800 and $1,200 with dignity if not comfort. Lachaise suffered some extraordinary professional expenses in those years but he nonetheless retained a preponderant proportion of his income for his family's living expenses, ranging in those years from $14,000 to nearly $30,000. Just having computed his recent record of earnings, Lachaise wrote to Isabel on Friday, no date (early thirties):

. . . between Sept. 15 last year and Sept. 15 this year—$24,750. So you see—don't be too anxious or discontent. It would be wise only to have saved aside a thousand dollars for days like these. But one can only be what one is. . . .

Early in the following year a letter reflects the effects of the depression and her despair in dealing with their problems; he replies:

I know the anxiety that you have; you know the difficulty of getting money but as you can see the money comes and in important sums after all. Instead of being sick it would be better to be content . . . and help Ed as much as one can. Ed has like others met many difficulties but he has like the rest of us many advantages. Like you and me as you can see. . . . (January 16, 1933)

Six months later, June 9, 1933, he replied again to a request for help and promptness by writing:

In answer to your last letter I cannot but repeat—a person who spends what you spend, with a man like me to give her money, should have a little patience with her difficulties when it's necessary to wait several hours for more money.

On July 11, Lachaise wrote to his stepson Edward Nagle:

. . . most of us are a thousand dollars too short! for comfort! or twenty cents too short—and yet life is still a song!

On May 27, 1934, Lachaise responded to a letter from Isabel saying:

I wrote to you yesterday of what had happened and that did not help too much with the pressing bills. I know how difficult it is to make the people that you owe patient and how that is disagreeable to meet and I am doing the best I can and as quickly as I can. I am giving you details of the money that we have received since May 25, 1933 for a year up until today, May 26, 1934, that makes in total $15,023.00. I know that you think that is very little—all the people that I am in contact with think that $10,000 is a very large and unusual income these days. The studio and the other expenses amount to $3,000 which leaves us $12,000 net income for the 12 months. I will be a little more patient in meeting my difficulties with money and with the heat. Love, Gaston.

On May 31, 1934, Lachaise receives a note informing him that Isabel wants to take a trip and that she has insufficient funds; he replies that he will send money as soon as possible.

. . . the only tragedy is that it is always several days late—I feel like the man who misses the train for Chicago by three minutes—and who runs after the train all the way—always three minutes late.

While Lachaise was considerate of Isabel's feelings and made every effort to provide for her in the way she felt appropriate, there were times when for reasons other than money matters, tensions would arise in their life. He might fail to be polite to a guest, or he might come late or not at all to an appointment because of his engagement in his work. Later he would apologize: "I am sorry that you are still mad at me, I am sure that you are fully justified to be so. . . ." (November 11, 1934.) At another point he writes, "If you think calmly you can comprehend 'myself' complicated and reaction to your complication and reach the bottom where you will find me as ever."

The Retrospective   In a number of letters to his wife during 1932 and 1933 Lachaise made reference to efforts on the part of Warburg and Kirstein to influence the decision-makers at the Museum of Modern Art to give a retrospective exhibition of Lachaise' work. In a letter of June 10, 1933, Lachaise reported to Isabel:

Saw Warburg. The exhibition will have to wait a year—in order to be done right. Goodyear insisting upon having other sculptors with me.[119]

A letter to Edward Nagle, dated June 9, 1934, says in effect that the Museum of Modern Art's decision regarding the retrospective show is about to be made and that there are several factions for and against him, with the supporting faction divided into those favoring a one-man show and those opting for a two-man show with either a painter or a sculptor, and William Zorach was specifically mentioned. Lachaise admits agreeing to the two-man show with a painter, but as to sharing the exhibition with Zorach, "To that I say no."

Somewhat later, an undated letter to Isabel reports, "I am naturally going to work to make the project succeed, but until the day of the opening arrives I won't believe it's true. . . ."

Writing Isabel on September 4, 1934, he philosophizes, "The Museum of Modern Art show for February has been announced. Now will be the struggle to make the show not too 'one side' the prudeur (stiff necked) and pretty leaping fishes and flying seagull side!"

Apparently at one point following the decision to announce the one-man retrospective, the assignment of the catalog essay was being discussed as to whether it should be written by the director, Alfred H. Barr, Jr., by a new staff member of the museum, Edward M. M. Warburg, or by Lincoln Kirstein. On October 5, 1934, a letter to Isabel from Lachaise gives the answer, "Kirstein came yesterday. Very happy about Philadelphia (the Art Alliance one-man exhibition, which was opening Nov. 27). He is busy at the catalog for the Museum show."

As late as December 22, 1934, in a letter to his stepson, Lachaise was still uncertain as to the general acceptance of his wishes for the exhibition, saying, "I am still very rushed in fact just now more than ever—I have to put a lot of fight all around on account of the coming exhibition which I am ready to throw overboard if I cannot have the way I want it."

Miss Dorothy Miller, at that time a staff member of the museum, and later its principal curator, recalled in 1951 that "Lachaise was afforded more freedom in his selection and arrangement of the show than any artist before or since." She claimed that when two or three crises arose in the development of the show, "Lachaise won on every issue." Miss Miller recalled Lachaise' conduct as exhibiting unhappiness and even an embittered quality, saying: "Mr. Barr tried to arrange and lead Lachaise but had to do so in a very subtle manner or he would receive Lachaise' full bitterness." [120]

It is plain from Kirstein's introduction to the catalog of the retrospective that Lachaise supervised the selection of works for the show, and that he had clearly thought through the question of showing "pretty leaping fishes," the architectural commissions, and the exploratory fragments and other works of erotic content, as Kirstein writes:

Lachaise has in his life done a great deal of work which, though he is by no means ashamed of it, he considers it to be of a secondary nature. This includes numerous decorative treatments of birds, fish and animals, all studied carefully for the fullest expression of their character but with full understanding of the slightness of the subject matter. It is not difficult to understand why these amiable objects have been widely popularized and even imitated. His architectural work of the past he also considers of a subordinate character. He always hoped for the day when he will be offered the chance to produce a work of sculpture in relation to architecture which is neither an apology for a blank wall or an incidental detail in the design. . . . [121]

In his own studio at present there are a number of pieces in plaster and bronze which have not been included in this retrospective exhibition. Lachaise feels these works to be of paramount importance to himself and the world's knowledge of him as an artist. If they were to be shown today, however, they might give offence and precipitate scandal obscuring the importance of the rest of his creation. . . .[122]

It then became clear that Lachaise obtained his show at the Museum of Modern Art almost entirely on his own terms. His reputation and his young friend's efforts combined to secure approval for the show over the opposition of the president of the museum. The selection of works was made primarily by the artist and his only restrictions were self-imposed ones in which the controversial and expressionist late works were omitted, but all sense of compromise with decorative work and commissions was ruled out. Finally, in the arrangement of the show, Lachaise prevailed over even the judgment and "subtle manner" of Mr. Barr. This was a very unusual success, inasmuch as it was the first one-man retrospective showing accorded a living American sculptor in the young history of the Museum of Modern Art. It was also unusual in that Lachaise did not conform to the readily publicized, clearly accessible, currently voguish School of Paris masterpiece genre that typified the early years of the museum's educational effort. Lachaise' show deliberately set out his strongest and most uncompromising material. It would be more than twenty-five years before a more complete exhibition would be undertaken, and even then, decorative "pretty fish" and unresolved architectural models diminished the effect even as new casts of the torsos and the late and final works added a more comprehensive view of the works of "paramount importance to himself and the world's knowledge of him as an artist."

The artist chose to show sixty sculptures and a lesser number of drawings—eighteen standing women; thirteen portrait heads, busts, and portrait figures; eight fragments and torsos; eight reclining figures, floating figures, and acrobats; and eight nonportrait heads based more or less on the head of Isabel. In addition a number of reliefs and seated figures, the *Man*, and the *Hand of Richard Buhlig* (Fig. 73) were included. Every one of the artist's major works—the *Elevation*, the *Floating Woman*, the *Heroic Woman*, *Man*, and *La Montagne Heroique* was shown. Every aspect of his serious work was well represented with examples which spanned the years and expressed the variety of his sculpture in the full scope of his twenty-five productive years in America.

The press notices were favorable. Henry McBride applauded the show in the *Sun* and pronounced Lachaise "the greatest of living sculptors." [123] The *Brooklyn Eagle* critic said ". . . eternal and elemental themes . . . and the life force are expressed in monumental conceptions." [124] The *Times* proclaimed him a "powerful and highly original sculptor." [125] Other reviews in the *Post*,[126] and *The New Yorker* magazine,[127] admitted the artist's technique, power, and skill while expressing reservations of one kind or another about the imagery and the expressive distortions in his work. Royal Cortissoz, writing in the *Herald Tribune*, mentioned ". . . a predilection for huge inflated forms. . . ." [128] Malcolm Vaughan, writing in the *American*, accused Lachaise of being ". . . an intellectualist . . . he has lost his humanity. . . . He is likely to thrust his own particular personality between you and the personality of his sitters." [129] Laurie Eglington, in *Art News*, had this to say, "True, his claim to greatness rests on a small proportion of the work shown, but of how many artists could this not be said? We must exclude from this group the portraits and the studies of men, in which field the artist meets with no success. His inspiration comes from the female aspect and divorced from this he gropes. . . ." [130]

Both Lachaise and Isabel were very pleased with the exhibition and the way it was displayed. Lachaise was extremely appreciative of Kirstein's considerable contribution, his loyalty and kindness. The exhibition was a triumph and at the age of fifty-three should have set the stage for twenty years of important work at the highest level of his own abilities and with ever-growing support from architects, civic leaders, and museum officialdom. It was, of course, not to be. The show, which opened January 29, 1935 and closed on March 7, five weeks later, was an official farewell, for within nine months Lachaise was dead of acute leukemia.

Within two weeks of his show's closing, Lachaise wrote to Edward Nagle, ". . . money still difficult to collect. About $5,000 I am claim by note, but which hard to cash. Don't worry about it—will manage it—yet I am trying not to give up sculpture too cheap. Spring and I had a birthday today— I am only fifty-three more years older than this very eternal young Spring."

By May he had finished the Rockefeller Center worker's reliefs and was waiting for his final check. He busied himself at a full life-size female nude in cement which has come to be called the *Garden Figure*. Then he returned to the Fairmount Park (Samuels Memorial) model, completing it before joining Isabel in Georgetown, late in May. In June he wrote again to Edward, saying "I am somewhat exhausted. . . ." Back in Georgetown on July 7, 1935, he wrote to Edward saying "Been here since Tuesday. Have to go to New York . . . Philadelphia this week . . . also the Nelson Rockefeller Mantel . . . I am wearing glasses now for reading, writing, or close work. 'great help.' " On August 8 he mentioned in another letter to Edward that "I have started a new group life size (lot of work)." Two days later he wrote again to Edward, "I have kept myself very busy both in the garden, the studio and the house . . . I have almost finished a life size group of *Dans la Nuit* if you do recall it and several small statuette from your mother . . . I am reading . . . 'Rembrandt' which show so far a happy luxurious life."

In October of 1935 Lachaise entered Mt. Sinai Hospital in New York City with the bleeding which began during a tooth extraction, and he died within four days. An initial diagnosis of leukemia has been debated; in fact his blood condition was such that the doctors could not save his life. While still accepting visitors, Lachaise said to Lincoln Kirstein's secretary, Mrs. Morris Fish, "I think this is very serious," [131] while to Isabel he spoke only of his love for her and of his admiration for his doctor's fine head, saying, "I must finish my work," and "I'd like to do that doctor's head." Each day he grew gradually weaker. There was no suffering, just increased weakness, and he did not talk about it. "We were neither of us religious. He was so brave in the last hours, he took it simply. Courage was the only way to meet his death. So he did it. We were both Catholics (but) his religion was myself and his work." [132] On October 18 he was dead.

The funeral was held on October 21, 1935 at the Frank E. Campbell "Funeral Church, Inc.," 1970 Broadway, New York City. Gilbert Seldes gave the eulogy. In an interview much later, Seldes said, "I was appalled when Madame Lachaise asked me to speak. Actually others were better fitted and I hadn't seen him for years. It was in the funeral home and there were only ten or fifteen people present. It was absolutely awful. Paul Rosenfeld and McBride were there. I said something about '. . . he has given us a new concept of what greatness is. . . .' " [133]

On the day of the funeral, McBride met Madame Lachaise as he approached the funeral home. He said, "I can't say anything. . . ." She replied, "You've said it all." Later he wrote for his paper:

The tawdry, ineffective funeral I would not have had otherwise. It was in the tradition. That's the way we buried Melville. That's the way we buried Poe. Greatness would not be greatness if it could be understood generally. Nor do I blame humanity of this poverty of vision nor cry out against God for it. It is merely the way things are.

Yet the word "genius" was uttered. There in a Broadway funeral "parlor" the word got uttered. Gilbert Seldes said it. Gilbert improvised a few words and set them to a note of bitterness. Yet the word "genius" was among them. That word will be remembered later. A great man passed from among us without the benefit of singing choir boys, without incense, without processions. . . . A few of us who knew that Gaston Lachaise was great sat there like wooden images in a Eugene O'Neill play and scuttled away the moment the crisp accents of Seldes ceased to be heard, to ruminate on greatness in America—and its recompense.

As far as Lachaise was concerned it might almost be said that of recompenses there were none, for genius is not truly paid with money, but with comprehension. Not but that there had been some admirers! There always had been a few. Perhaps the most notable was E. E. Cummings, the poet; himself so slightly acknowledged as to be practically of no use. Then there was Gilbert Seldes and later on Lincoln Kirstein and Edward Warburg.

It was probably due to the influence of the last named that the astonishing one-man exhibition of the Lachaise sculptures occurred in the Modern Museum last winter, an exhibition so overwhelming in its appeal that you would have thought that the whole world must have succumbed to it; but there were no signs of such a submission. Nothing from the collection was sold, and Lachaise told me himself that about all he got from the affair was my sympathetic account of it in *The Sun*. I do not repeat this boastfully but in despair. Were it not that I know that loftiness of feeling is never lost in this sluggish, unwieldy, careless but delightful old world of ours, and is unvariably recognized in the end, I should forever abstain from serious art criticism. . . .[134]

1. *Allys Lachaise in Traveling Costume*, Paris, c. 1905. Terra cotta. Whereabouts unknown.

2. *Woman with Turban*, c. 1910. Bronze, 10″ × 3¼″ × 5¾″. Lachaise Foundation.

II.

THE MAN and

HIS ART

Not a man to wait for inspiration, Gaston Lachaise was a prodigiously productive sculptor both in his own aesthetic purposes and in his work for other sculptors, his commissions, or portraits. His sculpture is complex and varied, and yet in the body of work that is most deeply personal there are recurring themes to which he returned obsessively. In order to examine the life work within a manageable context, this critical second section will be divided into eight categories: Standing Woman (Figs. 1–22), Portraits (Figs. 23–46), Reclining Woman (Figs. 47–56), Bas-Relief (Figs. 57–63), Acrobats and Floating Figures (Figs. 64–72), Fragments (Figs. 73–85), Groups; Lovers (Figs. 86–89), and The Late and Final Works (Figs. 90–95). It is intended that this technique may encourage comparisons within each category, between early, middle, and late examples as well as generalizations on the meaning of the work in the larger context of contemporary Western art. The artist's compelling frankness and obsessive concern with these recurring themes provides the viewer with an unusual opportunity for the study and understanding of this unique position in the art of modern sculpture.

Standing Woman

The standing woman is Gaston Lachaise' greatest contribution to world art. As Andrew Ritchie says, "His ideal of woman is different from Maillol's but they are both idealists nevertheless. Lachaise' Woman is of a similar order, however different in degree of voluptuousness to Maillol's peasant woman. . . . quite apart from influences, he is a great original genius, and one of the greatest to have worked in America." [1] It is important to recognize that Lachaise never did a nude in France. He restricted himself to portraits, genre figures, and animal pieces in his student days (Fig. 1). With the famed designer and jeweler Lalique, he produced jewelry, did commission work, and fashionable decorative arts assignments.

It was in Boston, while working for Kitson, that Lachaise first undertook the challenge of making a new nude, a twentieth-century Venus. He began, working in clay, on tiny voluptuous statuette figures, based upon his Isabel. His touch was as sure and as expressionist on the ten-inch figures as if he had modeled the nude for a lifetime. He had little in the way of facilities for working other than in small, and he pursued his modeling as he could, while commuting to Quincy and, thereafter, during the Boston days.

One of the earliest standing women we know, the *Woman with Turban*, c. 1910 (Fig. 2), measures only ten inches in height. This figurine strikes an elegant and commanding pose with its long dress, left arm on hip, right arm at side, holding her coat skirts back to reveal her supple figure, arched back, and proud bearing. The sculpture has a youthful vitality that likens it to Maillol's *Ile de France*. There is a transparency to the treatment of the dress which reveals the lithe sinuosity of the figure. It is a fully achieved statuette reflective of Lachaise' classical training and of his experience with Lalique.

Woman Arranging Hair, 1910–12 (Fig. 3), is a bold early piece, perhaps a more accurate reflection of the Boston *oeuvre* than is *Woman with Turban*. Not unrelated to the Armory Show figure or to a number of other prophetic statuettes of the period, it reflects a romanticism in its downcast head, cowl-like hair treatment, and sensual figure which emerges artfully from the disheveled drape. This is *his* model, his Isabel. We recognize her by her arched back, and the heavy up-turned breasts. The wide-legged stance, and the twisting of the torso, culminating in the raised arms with their hands plunged into the hair at the nape of the neck makes a powerful massing of energetic forms. The artist has worked from an image of his muse toward an emotional expression of feelings and then in the massings, twisting, and distribution of weights he has evoked a powerful symbol of feminine energy.

3. *Woman Arranging Hair*, c.
1910–12. Bronze, 10½″ × 5″ ×
3¾″. The Lydia and Harry Lewis
Winston Collection; Dr. and Mrs.
Barnett Malbin.

4. *Woman—Arms Akimbo,* c. 1910–12. Bronze, 11″ × 5″ × 5″. The Lydia and Harry Lewis Winston Collection; Dr. and Mrs. Barnett Malbin.

Another sculpture of the same period, *Woman—Arms Akimbo,* 1910–12 (Fig. 4), ripples with another motion: left leg forward, arms crooked with hands at the hips, a coat thrown over the shoulders, gathered around the arms, and floating behind. The pose suggests forward motion, head turned to the right, the torso and forward leg given sculptural life beneath the suggestion of a drape. The sculpture speaks of spontaneity and directness in its making. Lachaise' women were not destined long to avert their gazes or cast them downward, but soon, as he said, they would step out, ". . . moving vigorously, robustly, walking, alert, lightly radiating sex and soul. . . ." (finally) upstanding, noble, bountiful, poised on her toes, with closed, self-absorbed eyes, nearly detached from earth.

The standing *Woman* of 1912 (Fig. 5), is the sculpture Lachaise showed to Arthur B. Davies and Gutzon Borglum at the time of their visit to Kitson's Greenwich Village studio. With Kitson's permission Lachaise brought the plaster to their attention and it was invited to the Armory Show of 1913.[2] The 1912 sculpture has been amplified again, the figure is ever more bountiful and revealed through an open drape which is gathered at the left hip by that hand, while the right hand rests on the breast. The drape gathers below the knee into a tent shape from which the left calf extends. The rhythm of the movement from the gathered drape to the contraction at the knee, swelling out into hips, nude torso, turned head and touseled hair, is dramatic. Not only did Lachaise offer an unorthodox canon of physical beauty, but he cast it in an emotional format of unusual three dimensional virtuosity.

The foot-tall statuette of a woman called *La Force Eternelle,* 1913–18 (Fig. 6), is an elegant achievement in the statuette format. The now formalized draped figure stands firmly with left leg advanced, right arm behind back, left elbow raised to shoulder height with left hand at shoulder holding beads. The beads cascade down, around the left breast, into the draped area between the two widespread legs and return upward across the abdomen to the shadow of the right breast. The head turns to the left. The figure is in the tradition of the earlier statuettes but it is finished with an attention to surface, and a modeling of volumes that associates it more with Art Nouveau than with the bold and fauve-like handling of earlier statuettes. It must be noted that there is an orientalizing influence in the shaping of the face.

Woman, c. 1918 (Fig. 7), less than twelve inches in height,

5. *Woman*, 1912. Plaster,
10¾″. Lachaise Foundation.

is a figure which goes beyond the energy and naturalism of the early work. In it Lachaise appears to recognize that he had been moving consistently toward the establishment of a cult image of a female god figure. This work, whether consciously or not, represents that fulfillment. The tiny wimpled head with downcast eyes presides over a huge torso to which its arms are joined. The enormous mounded breasts and huge lower torso fall away to draped legs. The whole conveys a sense of tranquility and awesome power. It is truly a figure with religious overtones. Where the Armory figure (Fig. 5) and related pieces and *La Force Eternelle* (Fig. 6) are rooted in time, this piece has the timelessness of a totemic presence and could easily be the goddess of fecundity, a majestic giver of food and averter of famine, the keeper of the mystery of generative life.

The great American historian Henry Adams wrote: "The woman had once been supreme; in France she still seemed potent, not merely as a sentiment, but as a force. Why was she unknown in America? For evidently America was ashamed of her, and she was ashamed of herself, otherwise they would not have strewn fig-leaves so profusely all over her. When she was a true force, she was ignorant of fig-leaves, but the monthly-magazine-made American female had not a feature that would have been recognized by Adam. The trait was notorious and often humorous, but anyone brought up among Puritans knew that sex was sin. In any previous age, sex was strength. Neither art nor beauty was needed. Everyone, even among Puritans, knew that neither Diana of the Ephesians nor any of the Oriental goddesses was worshipped for her beauty. She was goddess because of her force; she was the animated dynamo; she was reproduction—the greatest and most mysterious of all energies; all that she needed was to be fecund." [3]

Sculpture has always been concerned with the nude female figure. The first "Venuses" go back more than 20,000 years before our time. The *Venus of Willendorf* (Fig. 8) often credited to be the earliest sculpture by man on earth, comes from the Aurignacian period of prehistory, and is surely the most fully plastic of Stone-Age Venuses. Her figure represents motherhood: the breasts, belly, and hips are exaggeratedly developed to emphasize their role in the eternal female's perpetuation of life. The thighs and lower legs are minimized through diminution. The figure's frail arms rest without gesture on the enormous breasts. The carving is not personalized but represents an unseeing primordial awareness of both the prehuman quality of sexuality and also the superhuman aspect thereof.[4]

The *Venus of Lespugue* (Fig. 9), dated somewhat later in

6. Opposite: *La Force Eternelle* (*Woman with Beads*), 1917. Bronze, 12½″ × 4″ × 5½″. Smith College Museum of Art; given by Stefan Bourgeois.

7. *Woman*, 1918. Bronze, 11½″. Lachaise Foundation.

the Aurignacian-Perigordian era, is carved in ivory. While Lachaise never referred to this or to other prehistoric Venuses in his letters, Kirstein wrote in the 1935 Retrospective's catalog: "The past he loves best is remotest, the very earliest dawn of European culture when men inscribed tusked mammoths and bison on the walls of their stone caverns, beasts with shaggy mountainous bodies delicately balanced on small, careful hoofs. Or small paleolithic objects carved from ivory or stone, female bodies of refined grossness, with huge mounded breasts capable of suckling whole tribes; earth goddesses which were in ten thousand years to be corrupted into the softer, many breasted Diana of the Ephesians. . . ." [5]

Reference must be made to the *Acrobat Woman* (Fig. 72) and her relationship to the Lespugue carving. It cannot be ignored that Lachaise was endeavoring to communicate about a matter of urgent significance to his own intellectual and emotional life. He was reaching into the archaic moat of humankind's experience to touch a foundation where man re-creates God in an image which is equally an homage to nature and a respect for the mystery of life. Lachaise knew that the caveman had a reverence, a craft, and a concept that was worthy of his sophisticated study and research. Lachaise was a man of quiet certainty and he built solidly upon knowledge and craft. He utilized every intellectual and emotional intuition to create arts of "barbarian impulse" [6] which were true to his experience. Like many another artist of the century, Lachaise knew that there was power and vitality in the "barbarian impulse," and he sought to understand it without neglecting or turning his back on the values, techniques, and refinements of his classical training and the role he was seeking to play in contemporary intellectual society.

The *Venus of Laussel* (Fig. 10), usually photographed as a flattened relief, is centered in the fertility shrine of her epoch. The figure is fully three dimensional in the reddish rock of the cave. One of the most vigorous sculptural representations of the human body in primeval art, the outward curve of the figure follows the surface of the stone outcrop—figure and block are inseparably interlocked. When viewed from the side, the block swells to the supreme point—the maternal belly. The whole body is polished, save for the head. It is also well known, in relation to the horn held in the right hand, that for some African tribes such a horn filled with blood is held to be the highest symbol of fertility.

8. Opposite top: *Venus of Willendorf,* c. 18,000 B.C. © by Prähistorische Abteilung, Wien.

9. Opposite bottom: *Venus of Lespugue* (Haute-Garonne), c. 18,000 B.C. Phototheque Musée de l'homme, Paris.

10. *Venus of Lausel,* c. 18,000 B.C. © by Achille B. Weider Fotografiker.

Deification of the female principle is not confined to the neolithic period. Fertility cult figures exist throughout the world and in widely separated periods. Europe, from Spain to the Caucasus, is one center. Pre-Columbian Mexico is another. There can be little doubt that "fertility worship" connected with a Mother Goddess cult must indeed be one of the oldest and longest surviving religions of the world. Surely the Venus of Willendorf and her sisters are "the earliest examples of human sculpture." [7]

Dancing Woman (Fig. 11), undated but conjectured to be 1915, stands 10⅞ inches tall. The figure dances, right leg extended, toes barely touching the base. The right arm is

11.   *Dancing Woman*, c. 1915.
Bronze, 10⅞″ × 3¼″ × 5¾″. Mr.
and Mrs. C. O. Wellington
Collection, New York.

12. *"Madame,"* no date.
Bronze, 7¼″. Mrs. Culver Orswell
Collection, Fogg Art Museum,
Harvard University.

extended backward and the left is raised, elbow on the level
of the shoulder with the forearm bent back, hand touching the chest below the neck. The treatment of the hair and
drapery is definitely within an art nouveau decorative tradition. The sculpture's sense of movement is vigorous, fully
pictorialized. The convention of tendrils of organic growth
being attached to a sculptural figure is followed with great
effect in summoning up the state of movement. It should be
recalled that in the teens Lachaise did a number of portrait
figures after Ruth St. Denis which the dancer admired at the
time, but she later came to deplore Lachaise' concern for
what she felt was his grotesque ideal. This figure could well
be a relic of the St. Denis studies or an adaptation therefrom.

Perhaps the least known figure of the early years is one
called *Madame* (Fig. 12) in the Orswell Collection. It is
undated, but stylistically it belongs to the 1910–19 period.
The figure stands on an irregularly shaped base, a nude figure

13. *Standing Woman with Arms behind Her Back*, c. 1918. Bronze, 13″. Collection The Fine Arts Gallery of San Diego, California; gift of Pliny Munger.

with a drape over the left shoulder, gathered at the mid-figure and falling around the left leg. The head is raised, turned to the right, the upper body shifts back to the left, nude to the waist. The right arm falls along the side with the forearm crossing the hip and disposing itself protectively in the pubic area. The undraped head, breasts, upper torso, right arm and leg, create a rhythm of bright reflection while the draperies pose a foil of darkness. The right leg extends itself away from the draped left leg and the aristocratic shape, placement, and tiptoed precision give the whole a sense of lyrical control that is unusual in any art, but especially in the intractable art of sculpture.

Standing Woman with Right Arm Outstretched, 1917–18 (Fig. 14), is a bronze that relates closely to a number of works discussed earlier, but it offers a firmly planted stance, a turning of the lower torso and head, a maintaining of posture by the upper torso. The right arm reaches out to the right in a dramatic gesture. The left arm extends and draws back from the elbow, holding a drape. The familiar goddess figure holds its central position, the left leg carrying the body weight, the right leg inclined toward the left knee, simplifying the silhouette and building toward the massing of incident in the upper section and the two gesticulating arm movements. The general feeling of the piece is that it has been caught in a stop-action camera photo, frozen forever.

The *Walking Woman*, 1922 (Fig. 16), is still another variation on the standing figure conception. In this celebrated work, the clothed figure strides forward in her ankle-length dress, making a membrane of bronze delineate the space between the two legs. The skirt swirls behind and all of the bright brassy metal is polished to a high brilliance. The right arm is held away from the body at the elbow and from that point the lower arm is raised in salute. The left arm is carried at extension behind in walking posture, with closed fist. The earth mother has been brought to the city, she walks among us, unrecognized. The finish may well owe something to Brancusi; the use of brilliantly polished surfaces was not normal to traditional sculpture and many artists preferred a patine of age. Lachaise was proclaiming his modernity in this finish and may well have been looking over his shoulder at Brancusi's *Bird in Flight, Torso of a Young Man*, or *Maiastra*. Lachaise spoke of "amplification and simplification" when he discussed developing an idea further with Reuben Nakian.[8] This nineteen-inch *Walking Woman* is in the tradition of Lachaise' earth mothers, but he has simplified

14. *Standing Woman with Right Arm Outstretched*, 1917–18. Bronze, 12″ × 6½″. Earl W. Grant Collection, San Diego Fine Art Gallery.

15. *Standing Nude*, c. 1921.
Bronze, 11¾″. Whereabouts
unknown.

16. *Walking Woman*, 1922.
Bronze, 19″. Julianne Kemper
Collection, Santa Monica,
California.

her appearance by eliminating details and marks of handling, finishing the work with a reflective polish which mirrors the environment and complicates the reading of the form.

Begun in 1912 in the room the artist kept on Washington Square South, the six-foot *Standing Woman* (*Elevation*; Fig. 17), was completed more than once in different studios before she was first shown in plaster at the 1918 Bourgeois show and finally cast in bronze for the Brummer Gallery, 1927. Such contemporaries as Stephan Bourgeois, Carl Van Vechten and Henry McBride [9] had always alleged that the figure *was* Isabel, Madame Lachaise. Nude photographs of Isabel from the earliest decade of the century in the files of the Lachaise Foundation, Boston, support the judgments of these friends and associates. The photographs reveal the carriage and proportions, the arched back, slender legs and the proud bearing. Of *Elevation* it is said that Lachaise brought the piece to a conclusion, destroyed it and made it over completely again prior to the Bourgeois exhibition. Comparing the handsome figure of the thirty-year-old Isabel with the finished sculpture serves to emphasize the adaptations of a master sculptor. Lifting the figure onto its toes, placing the weight on the left leg and extending the right, twisting the torso ever-so-slightly, forward with the left hip, down on the right hip, shoulders slightly to the left, arms raised in an ambiguous gesture of embrace, perhaps of self, with open palms. What had begun as an idealized portrait ended as the personification of the artist's vision of the female principle. Nearly detached from earth, she rises on her toes as a being different in kind. Her graceful, mannered feet and hands and fashionable legs lead our eyes to her ample child-bearing torso and the fruitful breasts of mother earth.

Standing Woman, 1912–27, called *Elevation* by Bourgeois, is the central work of Lachaise' productive life. Kirstein wrote of Lachaise in 1935 as: ". . . the interpreter of maturity . . . concerned with forms which have achieved their prime . . . the glory of their fulfillment." [10] She was his idol but he was not satisfied with depicting her as she appeared to the city but as a powerful presence, exuding sex and mystery, an inward looking divinity, presiding over creation and destruction. Lachaise passed beyond the superficial in idealizing his *woman*, transcending the temporal to achieve the archetypal which is, even when suppressed, a part of every human's experience. Seen in her wondrous, almost floating wholeness, *Elevation* represents the wisdom and idealism of a classic French-trained discipline transported

17. Opposite: *Standing Woman* (*Elevation*), 1912–27. Bronze, 70″. James G. Forsyth Fund; Albright-Knox Art Gallery, Buffalo, New York.

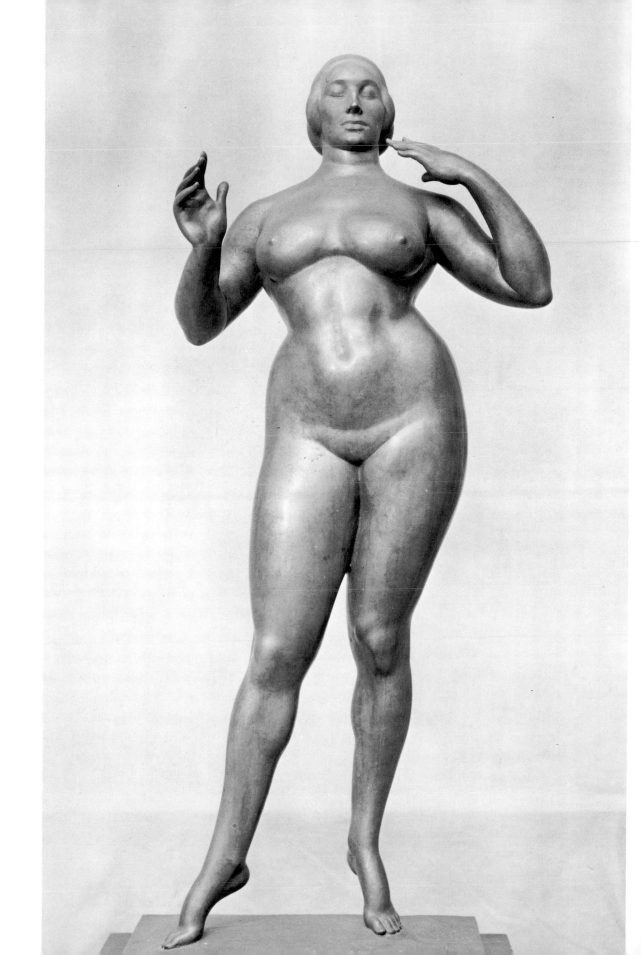

18. *Standing Woman with Pleated Skirt*, 1926. Bronze, 15¾″. Lachaise Foundation.

by physical love and emotionally realized intuition which has become American in spirit while still a part of the idol-building impulse of all races.

The stern figure of *Standing Woman with Pleated Skirt,* 1926 (Fig. 18), is recognizably the same subject with the carriage, stance, akimbo arms we have seen through fifteen years evolution. The figure is perhaps more full, with the hair comb, skirt and high-heeled shoe giving the piece a somewhat dated quality. Nonetheless, the work carries an awesome presence, a quality of majesty and unabashed potential.

Burlesque, 1930 (Fig. 19), was first cast in the early 1950s. It is one of the most difficult works of the artist in that it deals with a deformation rather than an amplification of the female figure, which does not occur in any other work. Lachaise enjoyed the circus, the burlesque, and the lively arts of the American twenties, often taking Mme. Lachaise to such entertainments. He could not make drawings in the darkened theatre but he was seriously impressed with the bumps and grinds of the show girls and their sexual magnetism. His *Burlesque* shows the right hand firmly clasped to her head, left arm gesturing high above her head as her left leg pumps out the grinding energy of the thrust which deforms her right hip, repeatedly. The dancer's closed eyes, her sense of concentration, effort, and even transport convey a message of ceremonial ecstasy, perhaps (of possession by) the experience of herself as the source of life.

Burlesque surely relates to the plastic fantasy of the *Acrobat Woman,* 1934 (Fig. 72 and No. 57 in the Museum of Modern Art's catalog). In that piece the ovals of hips, buttocks, shoulders, head, and breasts both merge and separate in an acrobatic expression of feminine wonder. While it is closely related to the earlier *Acrobat Woman,* 1929, in pose and thinking, it may also reflect an awareness of the *Lespugue Venus* (Fig. 9). That tiny ivory, slender in profile, but gigantic in its child-bearing sexuality recalls Kirstein's comment: "He feels that he is a link in the tradition of the handling of developed forms, but far more as a re-creation than as a reminiscence of previous epochs. . . ." Later Kirstein wrote: "He feels that the cavemen had already all the reverence, simplicity and fervor of subsequent 'great' periods, that their painting too had a majesty never revived in later inventions." "He admires the force of barbarians and feels there is not nearly enough of their directed impulse in art today." "He feels that his own work has a barbarian impulse which, taking nature as its base, makes nature idol-like

19. *Burlesque*, 1930. Bronze, 24½". Mrs. Culver Orswell Collection; Courtesy Fogg Art Museum, Harvard University.

20. *Standing Nude*, 1927. Chrome, black onyx base, 5⅜″ × 3¹⁵⁄₁₆″. The Alfred Stieglitz Collection; The Metropolitan Museum of Art.

21. *Woman in Balance,* 1927.
Bronze, 14″. Mrs. Culver Orswell
Collection; Fogg Art Museum,
Harvard University.

22. Opposite (and on jacket):
*Standing Woman (Heroic
Woman),* 1932. Bronze, 88½″.
Franklin D. Murphy Sculpture
Garden, University of California,
Los Angeles; gift of Mr. and
Mrs. Arthur C. Caplan, Mr.
and Mrs. Donald Winston, Mr.
and Mrs. Walter McC. Maitland.
Photo: Marvin Rand.

or godlike." [11] Surely *Burlesque* shares the mystery and ceremony of the later acrobat while touching natural phenomena with reverence, originality, and force.

The *Standing Nude* of 1927 (Fig. 20), is the last of the statuette series begun in Boston and continued in New York. This figure, closely related to *Standing Woman with Right Arm Outstretched* (Fig. 14) and *La Force Eternelle* (Fig. 6), carries its weight on the right leg, with the left extended. The right arm is tucked behind her back with only the elbow and the drapery held by it showing, the left arm rests on the hip with hand closed. The hips shift slightly to the right, while the shoulders move to the left and the head follows the shoulders even more markedly. The drapery, hair, nipples, and pubic areas are finished in dull bronze while the main figure has been plated with chrome. The figure is recognizably Mme. Lachaise again, with her impassive composure but also with a sense of exuberance and celebration of herself.

The *Heroic Woman*, 1932 (Fig. 22), is surely the triumph and fulfillment of all Lachaise' small studies, statuettes, and fragments. Unlike *Elevation* (Fig. 17), the figure takes a firm stance, holds her head high and places her hands determinedly on one hip and another thigh. It is a regal pose, one of composure and force. The sculpture is the embodiment of Lachaise' life-long effort to express the imperious goddess quality in the heroic scale. Here he has achieved it with unhesitating completeness. As Hilton Kramer has said: "Nowhere in Lachaise's *oeuvre* is his favored conception of the female figure—with the breasts and arms, the thighs and buttocks and belly forming a centrifugal orchestration of masses around the delicate, slender waist—given a more complete realization." [12]

Portraits

From his earliest years, Lachaise had worked with the tools of his father in the shops in Paris and the suburbs. He had become aware of woodworking tools and techniques, learned to work in plaster for moldings, and to make ornamental decorations for the interiors of homes and the private rooms at the top of the Eiffel Tower. He was thus particularly prepared for the work at the Ecole Bernard Palissy, where clay modeling, plaster and bronze casting, and stone carving were the center of the sculpture curriculum. He studied with the director M. Aube and with the master in sculpture M. Moncel, who himself had studied at the Beaux-Arts and was a known neoclassicist. His preparation at the Ecole and the high recommendations of M. Moncel facilitated his early admission to the Académie Nationale des Beaux-Arts in 1898. It was Lachaise' privilege to be accepted in the studio of Jules Thomas, a highly reputed neoclassicist, in the principal studio of the three devoted to sculpture at the Beaux-Arts. That year Lachaise modeled a portrait bust of his sister Allys which is sweetly precocious (Fig. 23). The head is slightly tilted, turned a bit to the right, with keenly observed bone structure and an unpretentious, youthful life to the neck, chin, and cheeks. The coiffure is bouffant, piled high and leaving the head structure revealed. It reflects classic models but has a romantic overtone in the suggestion of dreaminess about the subject's gaze. It is a remarkable portrait but all the more so from an artist of such a tender age.

In later years Lachaise acknowledged to his stepson, Edward Nagle, that he had a great regard for the French naturalist sculptor of portraits, Jean Antoine Houdon (1741–1828), generally considered to be the greatest portrait sculptor of his time. At the Beaux-Arts Lachaise studied Greek and Roman casts at school, drawing and modeling from them and from live models, and he visited the Louvre, the Musée des Arts Décoratifs, the Cluny Museum, examining Roman portrait busts as well as contemporary works. This was the time of Auguste Rodin (1840–1917) and his romanticism, individualism, and preference for modeling could not but affect the climate of art study for Lachaise. It was also the age of *Art Nouveau* aestheticism, and the sinuous and decorative stylization of natural growth forms over extended surfaces. Finally, this was also a period of discovery in the ancient and primitive arts; and the New World's arts, those of the Orient, the Hindu, the Egyptian, and even the caveman were becoming known and Lachaise was open to their powerful energies, their expressive influence.

In his own practice at the Beaux-Arts, either working from the plaster replica of Roman antiquity or from the model, Lachaise was in touch with a finely geared factual recording of the sitter. He came to render the most fugitive of facial expressions as well as the most prosaic ones. Each subject was seen as he was through the filter of Roman portraiture. Romanticism, Rodin, Art Nouveau, and the dramatic example of Houdon's naturalism coexisted in the consciousness of the young student. At times he worked very hard and with utter respect for his master. At other times

23. *Portrait of Allys Lachaise,* 1897. Bronze, 16″. Collection The Museum of Modern Art, New York; gift of Allys Lachaise.

24. *Head of a Woman (The Egyptian Head)*, 1923. Bronze, 13½″. Collection of The Newark Museum; gift of Mr. and Mrs. Feliz Fuld.

25. Opposite: *Head of a Woman*, 1923. Polychromed, mottled marble, 27.3 cms. Courtesy Museum of Fine Arts, Boston; gift of Margarett Sargent McKean in memory of Nathaniel Saltonstall.

he worked rather lazily, studied in the museums, attended the studio parties, visited the *Bal Musette*, the *Concerts Rouges*, sat in the parks and read the poetry of Baudelaire, Rimbaud, and Verlaine. He was quickly recognized as a specially gifted younger artist. His *Allys* was shown at the Salon of 1898. Twice he was chosen in the first twenty of three hundred students to compete for the Prix de Rome. He exhibited frequently at the *Salon des Artistes Français*.

From those early years Lachaise found that he enjoyed doing portraits of people he admired. He portrayed his sister Allys and his mother on numerous occasions. When he met Mrs. Nagle he invited her to pose after their second meeting. The conflict between the ideal and the real began at this time in his career and was forever a part of the tension in his art. Men could be depicted in the Roman-Houdon classical line as they were, without searching for the characterizing gesture but with full awareness of the mystery of the expression of human character. With the portrait of women, however, Lachaise moved into a different field. In a number of works that can only be called portraits he found himself producing imagined works of a female type, undoubtedly related to states of mind based in his observation of Belle, but nonetheless idealized, built up from the structure of classical portraiture but imbued with the romantic sensations and intuitions of an artist searching for his unique expression of truth in his own human experience.

The Egyptian *Head of a Woman*, 1923 (Fig. 24), is perhaps the earliest fully mature and completely realized example of Lachaise' idealism. It is a depiction of his wife Isabel as his muse. Her head and hair and neck carry the message of her full figure, her ample proportions, and his loving admiration for her. The eyes are closed, the head is tilted to the left, the face is in repose and the asymmetric massing of the coiffure gives movement to the tranquility of the pose. The neck swells unnaturally as a plastic reflection of the patinated hair and the balance of the whole piece. The forms are full, the lips sensuous, the profile personalized. Lachaise' forms are filled with life, Isabel forever in peak maturity is expressed in all of her outgoing physical majesty and her inward exploration of her feelings and her essence.

The stern, even dour *Head of a Woman*, 1923 (Fig. 25), in mottled pink marble with patinated hair (at the Museum of Fine Arts in Boston and in bronze elsewhere) is one of the most memorable heads based on Mme. Lachaise' portrait; but it is imbued with that idealism which transfigures time.

The head is set, firmly staring ahead. The resolution of the mouth is determined, even harsh, the set of the jaw is more than resolute, nonetheless the lips and the jaw give powerful energy to the large proportions of the head, the broad cheek planes, the powerful disposition of hair masses, the unifying piling and rolling of volumes which is so typical of the period in his art. This work is based upon the strong-minded force of Isabel and her mature beauty but is idealized beyond that into an expression of female energy and determination and the physical power to see any task through to its fulfillment. Each plane moves surely into its congruencies with every other plane, falling away, blending into others with compound relations. "Sculpture is entirely (the) *relation* of forms," Lachaise told George L. K. Morris, while working on the painter's portrait bust, "which flow in an unending belt through a head, a neck, a torso; and they must all go together, a foot must (go) with a head in the same figure." [13]

In the *Mask of Marie Pierce*, 1924 (Fig. 26), one finds Lachaise operating at the peak of his portrait powers. There is an objectivity about this portrait that is quite different from the more generalized and awesome power of the 1923 *Head of a Woman* (Fig. 25). Lachaise felt a great sympathy for Marie, a niece of Isabel, and spoke of her as the most beautiful woman he had ever known. The work was modeled in clay, cast in plaster and then in bronze. The bronze was worked to high finish and then nickel-plated. The mask form is not usual in portraiture but is in fact one of Lachaise' contributions to American portrait sculpture. The fragmentary quality of the piece, summoning up the missing halo of hair as well as the whole female figure is a powerful communication of the potentialities of portrait sculpture. The mature, composed face mask, merging into the firm chin and neck line, executed in the machine-tool precision of nickel has a refinement as well as a toughness, a humanity as well as a likeness, and an inwardness of touching quality. The *Mask of Marie Pierce* is more than a likeness. Like a Roman or even an Egyptian portrait it summons up more than the woman, it recalls her epoch as well. *Marie Pierce* radiates a vital expression of life and beauty as well as a somewhat somber awareness of their fragility.

Lachaise made portraits of many of the pacesetters of American intellectual society, including a number of the distinguished group surrounding *The Dial* magazine. He did portraits of Scofield Thayer (Fig. 37) and James Sibley

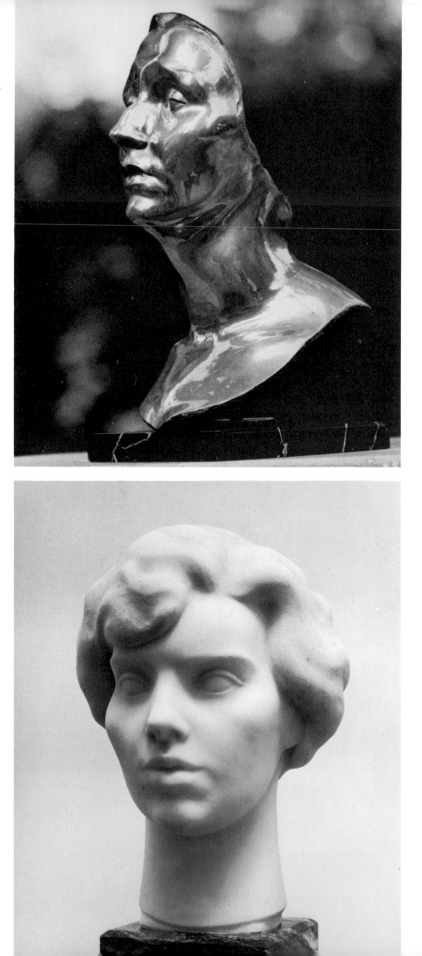

26. *Mask of Marie Pierce,* 1924. Nickel plated bronze, 14⅞″ × 7⅛″. The Denver Art Museum; gift of Mr. and Mrs. T. Edward Hanley.

27. *Antoinette Kraushaar,* 1923. Marble, 13½″. Antoinette Kraushaar Collection, New York.

Watson, Jr. (Fig. 30), the copublishers of the magazine, and
of Henry McBride (Fig. 35), *The Dial*'s art critic, also of
M. R. Werner, the writer, Hildegarde Watson, wife of the
publisher, Gilbert Seldes, associate and managing editor, and
his family (Fig. 39), and E. E. Cummings (Fig. 28), just to
name a representative cross-section. Three portraits of distinguished artists help to give special insight into the artist
and his working procedures.

Lachaise generally worked with a plasticene foundation
which he prepared on his own armature. Usually his sitters
came for one hour sittings (between ten and seventy times)
during which he worked quite feverishly, beating the plasticene with a hammer, measuring the visitor's skull or individual features with calipers, working with both hands,
very swiftly. In more than a dozen cases sitters have reported that he got a striking likeness on the first visit, only to
destroy it and begin again at the next visit. Marianne Moore
(Fig. 29) remembered that Lachaise asked her in *The Dial*
office if she would pose for him. She told him that she
was not a good subject. He told her "It does not matter what
you weigh, it is the spirit that counts. . . . You have charm.
. . . You have a good ear." She reported that he was solicitous
to have her pose the way she wanted to look and that he took
great pains to arrange her hair and hair pins in a manner
she found acceptable. Miss Moore had only six sittings and
the work was not "finished" because her mother became ill
and she was unable to make the journeys to the studio. It
was only years later, after Lachaise' death, that Lincoln
Kirstein arranged to have the plaster cast in bronze and
presented to Miss Moore. She recalled that the original in-
tention was to have the work pointed up in marble and to
have the hair red.[14] The head rises on the slender, sprightly
neck, a capsule of crowded life, objectively described and yet
with a special sense of audacity, as though this sitter has a
rashness which hides within her modesty, a boldness that is
not entirely veiled by her apparent prudence. The artist's
handling is not merely more expressive than in the Marie
Pierce, it also bespeaks a spontaneous unfinishedness which
gives the work great vitality. Miss Moore recalled that on
one occasion in *The Dial* office he had said to her "I have all
I can do to keep my boat from sinking." She remembers her
unspoken sense of objecting to "the extremes to which he
went in his heavy torsos, distorted and overemphasized." At
the same time she recognized "that he was kind, direct, very
stubborn." She said "It would be impossible to do justice to

28.   Opposite: *E. E. Cummings,*
1924. Bronze, 14½″. Estate of
Marion M. Cummings, Fogg Art
Museum, Harvard University.

29.   *Marianne Moore,* 1924.
Bronze, 14¾″. The Metropolitan
Museum of Art, New York.

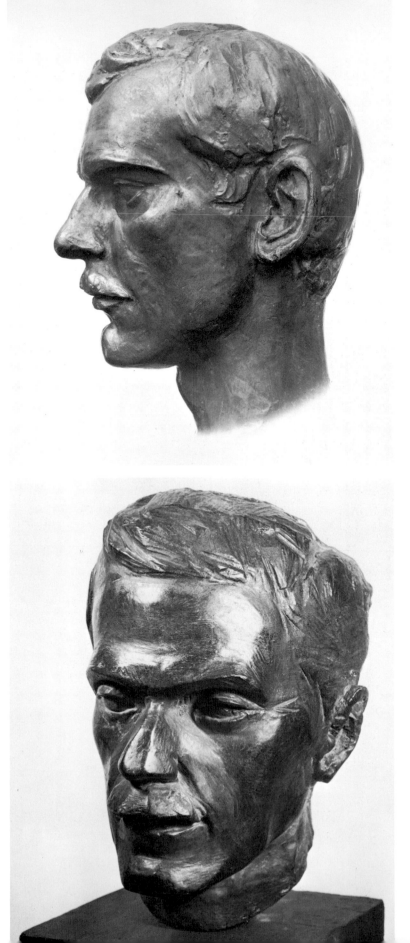

30. *Dr. James Sibley Watson,*
Jr., 1927. Bronze, 15″. Dr. J. S.
Watson, Jr. Collection, Rochester,
New York.

31. *Alfred Stieglitz,* 1928. 14″.
Plaster. Lachaise Foundation.

Lachaise' kindness. . . . if he hadn't been almost uncommonly stubborn he might not have been the sculptor he was. I didn't realize what a symbol he is of integrity. I did perceive his congenital inescape from adversity—in a way his character was wrought by adversity. His was a dissent to the world of compromise." [15]

We know from a number of sources (Mme. Lachaise, Werner, Cummings) that Lachaise had great feeling for John Marin's work and for him as a human being and fellow artist. The bust of Marin (Fig. 32) was executed in 1928 with an expressionist boldness that is the most free and inventive of any Lachaise portraits; at the same time it is a daring likeness which explores the psychology of the subject. He enjoyed representing people he admired; working quickly he got astonishing likenesses only to redo them at the beginning of the next sitting. Perhaps it was because of his intense admiration for Marin that he moved to a less objective but more artful likeness growing out of his sense of Marin's suffering, and once he recognized what he had, he stopped. This bust is perhaps the most famous American portrait of the century. (Eleven of the twelve casts are in American museums.) Lachaise spoke of the bust, saying that

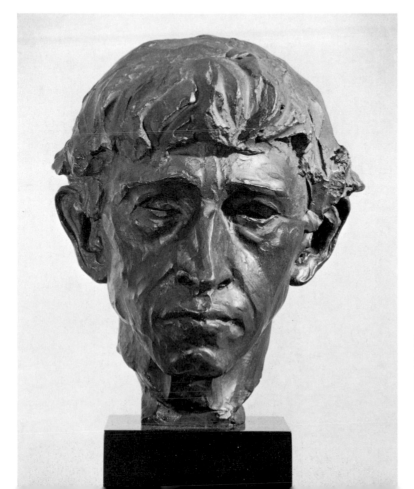

32. *John Marin*, 1928. Bronze, 12″. Des Moines Art Center, James D. Edmundson Purchase Fund.

33. *Georgia O'Keeffe*, 1927.
Alabaster, 23″. Collection of the
Metropolitan Museum of Art;
The Alfred Stieglitz Collection.

it was "the face of a man who had suffered, sacrificed and triumphed without vanity." [16] The finish of the piece is an unassuming one, utterly without adornment, essential, and in keeping with the craggy honesty of John Marin.

Lachaise did not ordinarily agree to do a portrait unless he admired the sitter. He did often feel financial pressures and he sometimes relented, but it was always unwillingly and he did not know how to be completely acquiescent about it. Lachaise didn't like Georgia O'Keeffe, but he felt indebted to Alfred Stieglitz (Fig. 31) and agreed to do her portrait (Fig. 33). Lachaise felt it was better to pay for a show than to be under obligation to a dealer. Stieglitz had bought pieces and O'Keeffe herself did so later in the twenties; at any rate Lachaise felt it was impossible to avoid doing her portrait. The 1926 portrait in alabaster is twenty-three inches tall, which is large in Lachaise' work. It is clear from the piece that he has treated her coldly and that he feels that quality in her demeanor and appearance. The nearly grainless white stone has a chill of reserve about it that clearly shows Lachaise did not feel sympathy for his subject. There is a cruel truth about the work that reflects his feeling that "she was flashy" and a careerist. He had told Stieglitz that he would not "work for her"—a condition Stieglitz sought to extort from Lachaise at the time they were planning the 1927 exhibition at the Intimate Gallery. There is an objective depiction of forms and a clarity of imagery that is unmistakably a likeness; at the same time there is a hardness, a boldness about the face, the cheeks, and the profile that communicates the feeling that to his eye this is not a feminine person: strong and willful perhaps, but not compassionate.

Edward M. M. Warburg, close friend of Kirstein and supporter of the Harvard Society for Modern Art, became a patron of Lachaise in the thirties and bought a number of works of unusual quality. Despite his support, Lachaise was slow to warm to Warburg, perhaps feeling that the extremely handsome and moneyed young man was frivolous. Lachaise did not show an interest in doing a portrait until he had known him for five years. The piece was contracted for in 1932, begun in clay and pointed up in alabaster (Fig. 41). Warburg recalls more than fifty sittings. On the first day it was complete in the clay. "Actually there were fifty different portraits all valid but unsatisfactory to Lachaise." [17] The artist was very intense about his work and even on the trip by train to White Sulphur Springs he modeled and studied the bust. He stayed on at the Springs for nearly a week in 1933 working every day with sittings at least twice daily.

34. *Edgard Varèse*, 1928.
Plaster, 16½″. Lachaise
Foundation.

35. Opposite: *Henry McBride*,
1928. Bronze, 13½″. Estate of
Henry McBride, Collection, Museum of Modern Art.

36.   Opposite: *Mask*, 1928.
Lead, 6¾″ × 5¾″. Cincinnati Art
Museum, gift of Dr. and Mrs.
J. Louis Ransohoff.

37.   *Scofield Thayer*. Bronze,
12¹³⁄₁₆″ × 6⅞″ × 8¾″. The Dial
Collection, Worcester Art Museum, Massachusetts.

38. *Carl Van Vechten*, 1931.
Nickel plated bronze, 15½″.
Courtesy of The Art Institute of
Chicago.

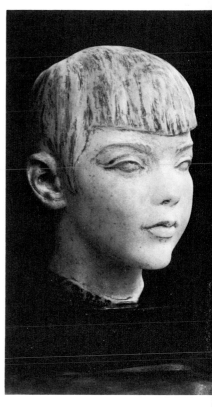

39. *Timothy Seldes*, 1931. Pink marble, 10½". Mr. and Mrs. Timothy Seldes, New York.

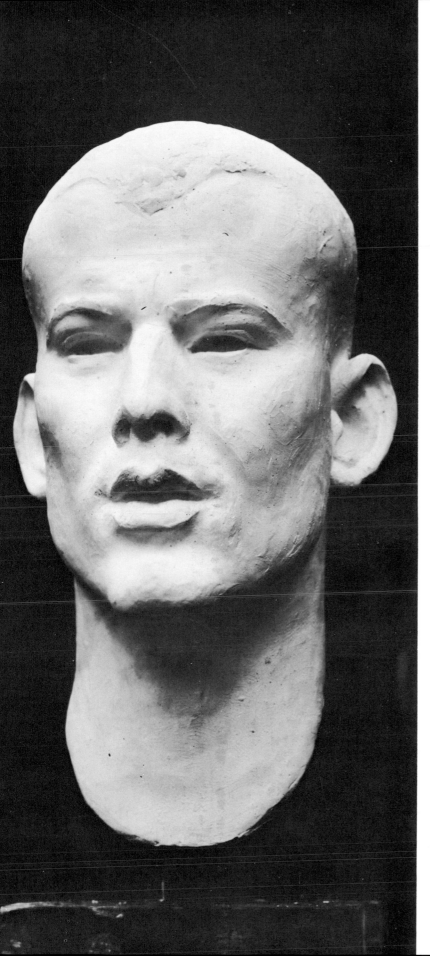

40. *Lincoln Kirstein*, 1932. Plaster for bronze, 15½". Mr. and Mrs. Lincoln Kirstein, New York.

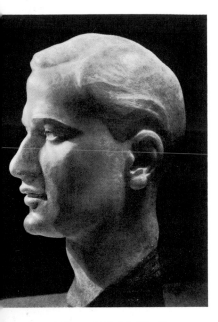

41. *Edward M. M. Warburg,*
1933. Alabaster, 14½″. Mr. and
Mrs. Edward M. M. Warburg,
New York.

42. *George L. K. Morris,* 1933.
Marble, 32″. Mr. and Mrs.
George L. K. Morris, Lenox,
Massachusetts.

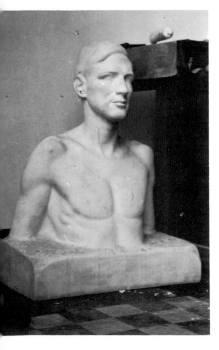

Henry McBride claimed that "a portrait sculpture is a depiction where there is always something the matter with the mouth." In Warburg's case he felt it was something wrong with the nose. He felt that "the nose was too high on the head, not the Semitic two-thirds but Roman proportions." It is a remarkable sculpture, however, not merely for the beauty of the precious materials and the craftsmanship, but for its visual clarity and intensity. Lachaise judged the work in retrospect to be among his very finest portraits—one that might be measured against the best of any period.[18]

Lachaise' process was to pose his model and work with the likeness until he felt that he had touched the truth of the person. He worked not for the likeness as much as for "a likeness with the skin removed,"[19] where he had an essence of the person. The moment to stop working seemed to coincide with his feeling that formally he had achieved a plastic reality that was also sculpture: he had made a portrait but also a Gaston Lachaise.

Lachaise was unique in his concern for the nude portrait in sculpture. Few of his patrons were prepared for the idea of a nude portrait, but several were bold enough to undertake the project. Lincoln Kirstein and Lachaise found an Egyptian pharaoh in gold, six inches tall, in the Metropolitan Museum of Art and together hit upon the idea of doing a portrait of Kirstein after the diminutive god-king (Fig. 44).

The youthful figure of the boxer-dancer-intellectual strides forward on his right leg, chest high, head alert, arms held as though carrying the emblems of office and the symbols of power. The figure has an elastic grace that is very alive. The hands and arms seem to be invested with ceremonial meaning. It is not a "speaking" gesture which Kirstein holds but one of perhaps forgotten art meaning. It might remind one of the "embracing" gesture of the *Standing Woman,* 1912–27 (Fig. 17), where the arm posture gives added presence to an already imposing image. It is as though a Greek bronze athlete of the fifth century B.C. had taken a longer stride, holding a more inward sense of himself in serving some important mission. The delineation of musculature and skeletal structure is less specific than in either of the portraits of G. L. K. Morris (Figs. 42, 45): naturalism is tempered in a work invested with clear importance by the artist. Beside this sculpture all of Lachaise' particularized male figures are merely objective: the Goodwin marble of 1927, the *Male Acrobat* and the *Athlete,* both of 1928, are exercises of an ambitious technician as

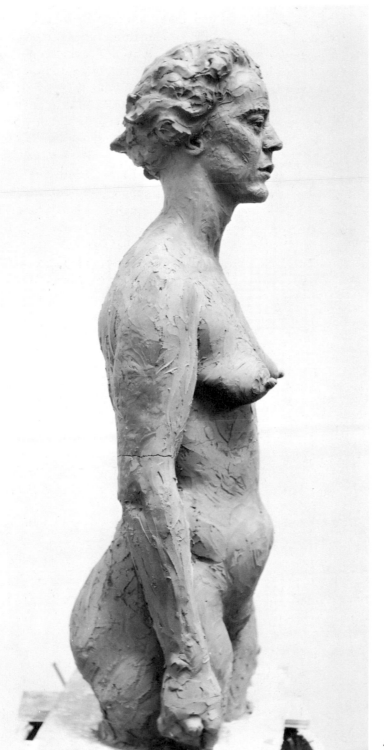

43. *Portrait figure,* 1934–35.
Plaster for bronze, 45″. Lachaise
Foundation.

44. *Man Walking* (*Portrait of Lincoln Kirstein*), 1933. Bronze, 23¼″. Collection of the Whitney Museum of American Art, New York.

45. *Boy with a Tennis Racket,*
1933. Bronze, 23″. Mr. George
L. K. Morris, Lenox,
Massachusetts.

-distinguished from a master sculptor challenged by a great theme. The *Portrait of George L. K. Morris* in marble is fully seen, as is the full figure portrait *Boy with a Tennis Racket* (Fig. 45)—both 1933—and yet they are not lifted out of their own time into the history of sculpture as he sought to do in his most ambitious and fully realized portraits.

The Man

Madame Lachaise was certain that the Kirstein commission vitalized Lachaise' interest in doing the male heroic figure, which had been begun in 1930, but was not finished until two years after the Kirstein *Walking Man*. Lachaise had said in 1928: "Of late a vision of the form of MAN is growing more clear and precise to me. I must (begin to) attempt to realize it. Undoubtedly he will be the son of WOMAN." [20]

The *Man* poses problems (Fig. 46). He lacks the elegance, the levitation, the refined extremities of the *Standing Woman* (Fig. 17). It is as though Lachaise compared his own physical being to the buoyant figure of his Isabel. Where her spirit soared, he felt himself to be earthbound. Where she was life in every detail or fragment, he knew himself to be the worker, the sweaty, heavy limbed, thick fingered, overly-strong protector.

Probably both the heads of his stepson Edward Nagle and the portrait bust of Lincoln Kirstein had an influence on the *Man*'s head, but most importantly the sense of freedom Lachaise found in the *Walking Man* kept him working at this figure through the six long years of its development. One must recognize that the artist evoked a sense of dignity, or *presence* in the 8½-foot figure with its outstretched arm and reaching hand which suggests calm, confidence, reassurance, protection, strength in reserve—incarnations of the manly virtues.

The Reclining Woman

The reclining female figure was an early subject which with the passage of years became one of the artist's important and obsessive themes. Perhaps the earliest known work in the genre is the portrait of his mother (1903?), estate of Allys Lachaise. This sculpture poses the seated figure with both feet touching the floor, legs slightly separated under the floor-length skirt, arms on the supporting chair arms, shoulders and head turned slightly to the right, resting upon the back of the supporting chair. This use of furniture as a

46. Opposite: *Man*, 1930–34. Bronze, 102″. Chrysler Museum at Norfolk, Virginia; gift of Walter P. Chrysler, Jr.

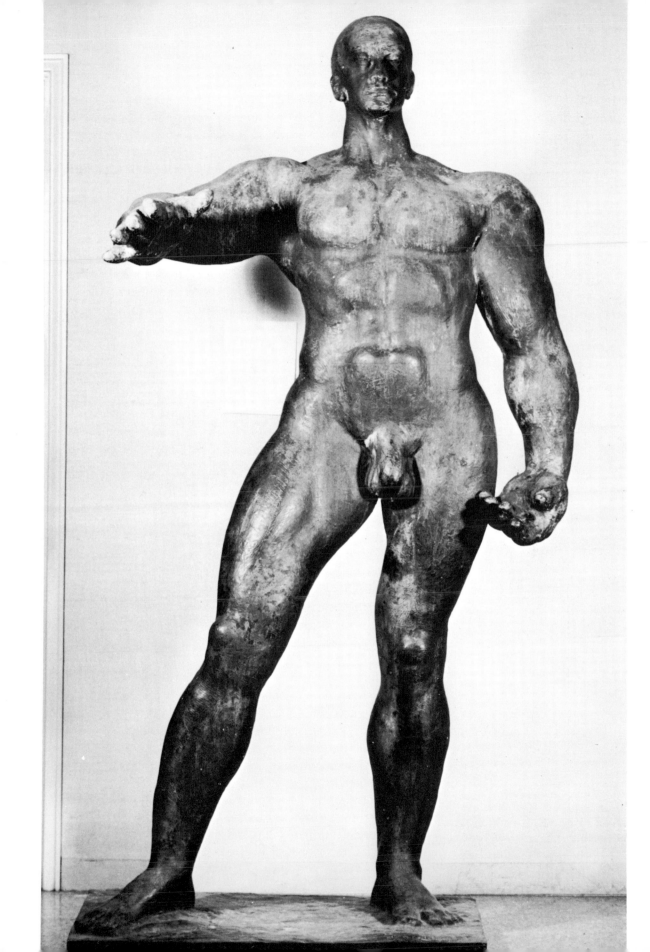

part of the piece is not an unusual convention for end-of-the-century French academism, but it is seen only sparingly in Lachaise' work. The posture of the figure suggests simultaneously repose, physical tiredness, and mental alertness. There is a genre-like quality of folk art about the chair and figure, but the refined, sweet portrait head has unquestionable art quality.

Lachaise explored an entirely different aspect of the reclining female figure in the tiny sleeping nude in plaster known only in photograph (Fig. 47).[21] This figure, measuring a scant seven inches, is posed on its right side, with legs drawn up in near fetal position, arms folded under the head. The full figure suggests the artist's mature ideal and yet the pose is never duplicated in his single figure work.[22] The piece probably dates from before 1910. The informality and touseled romantic quality of this lyric work may well mark the earliest suggestion of the theme of the female mountain in Lachaise' art.

The *Woman on a Sofa*, (1918–23) (Fig. 48), presents the fully clad figure reclining on a chaise, with two pillows piled up beneath her shoulders, feet extended over the end of the chaise, shod in a shaped-heel pump. The figure's rounded breasts are draped with a shawl or coverlet. The head, severely coifed, turns to the right with an austere composure. The right arm rests on the chaise with the hand in a somewhat mannered posture. This is a depiction of a commanding and secure female.

Woman on a Couch, 1928 (Fig. 49), in the Joseph Hirshhorn collection, is a variant on the theme of the previous sculpture. The artist may well have adapted a plaster cast of the earlier piece, in the manner of Rodin.[23] While this sculpture is dated five years later, the artist has retained the chaise, figure, the posture of the torso, and the legs as they were in the earlier piece. The head, however, is tipped forward, the face is more generalized, and the eyes gaze toward the now extended right hand which is posed, spread-fingered, as though holding a book. The work, in its final state, appears to catch the artist's wife in an informal moment, reading, perhaps aloud, from her encyclopedic collection of contemporary prose and poetry, or perhaps from her own poetry.

Both of the figures reclining on a chaise deal with the full figure in the twenties domestic scene. The quality of the grande dame is firmly carried in the bearing, figure, and carriage of the head. What may be diluted in the second

47. *Foetal Figure*, before 1910. Plaster, 2⅜″ × 4½″ × 2½″. Allys Lachaise Collection.

48. Opposite top: *Woman on a Sofa*, 1918–23. Plaster, 9¼″. The Museum of Modern Art, New York.

49. Opposite bottom: *Woman on a Couch*, 1928. Bronze, 9½″ × 16″ × 10½″. The Hirshhorn Museum and Sculpture Garden, Smithsonian Institution.

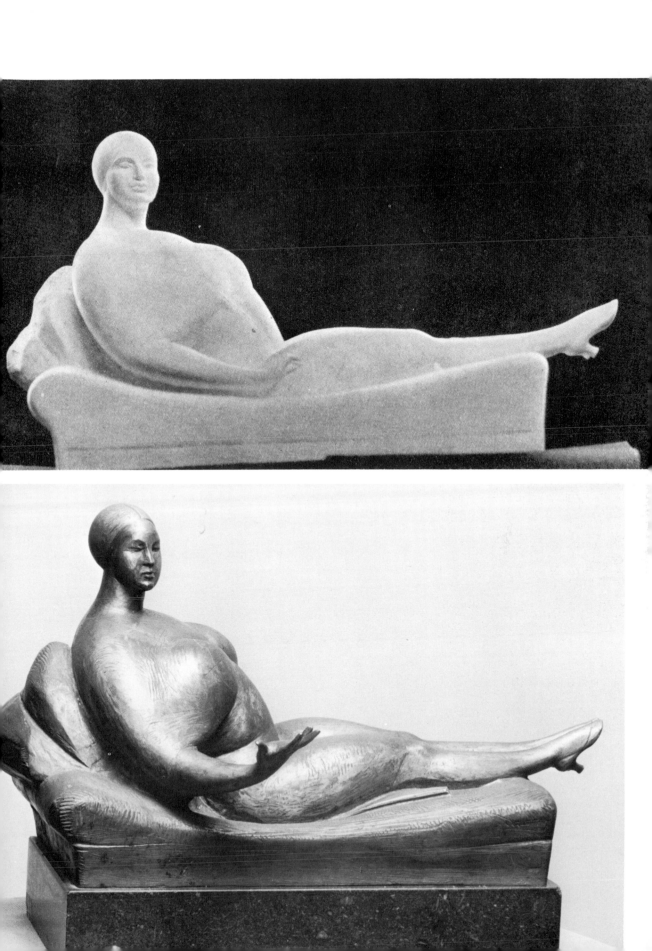

50. *Reclining Woman*, 1919. Bronze, 11½″ × 20″. Mitzi Landau Collection, Los Angeles.

piece's inclined turbaned head is regained in the imperious gesture of the arm and hand. Whether in regal composure or in casual reading this is a forceful spirit, a powerful presence.

One of the most compelling and influential of Lachaise' reclining nudes is the figure of 1919 (Fig. 50). This is a naturalistic interpretation of refinement and elegance. The figure rests on its right hip, the upper torso raised and supported by the right arm. The left leg crosses the right leg in a generous and feminine gesture. At the same time the left arm extends itself along the left hip, echoing the gesture and direction of the leg, with the hand opened outward, the thumb spread. The visage of the figure is severe, stylized, unsmiling; the banded coiffure like a helmet. While the full-blown figure reclines sensuously and the left leg reaches outward expressively, the left hand shows its palm as if in invitation, in contrast to the stern self-discipline of the visage which dominates the earthy figure. It should be mentioned that the work is like all of the important Lachaise figures in that the head is not in the Greek proportion to the whole figure— it is smaller, emphasizing the powerful generative mysteries of the female body and (at the same time) suggesting the peculiar genius of the mind's relative weight to the powerful animal forces of life and its disciplinary wonder.

The lean, classical head assumes a dour power not dissimilar to an oriental religious sculpture. The heavy belly and breasts reflect femininity; at the same time there is a youthfulness and muscular potency which is evident. The graceful long legs with their tiny feet are in keeping with the artist's oeuvre, though seen here only in the prototype of *The Mountain* (Figs. 53–56). The bending of the figure's arm in supporting the massive weight of the torso corresponds to the palpable weightiness of breasts and belly. Overall the figure conveys an all-powerful pride in its sexual self, the amplitudinous torso of mother earth, through the self-supporting arm, the carriage of the head. Rounded forms tend to carry the suggestion of fruitfulness, maturity. Women's breasts can serve as metaphors for fecund pastures, and most fruits tend to be rounded. Lachaise has relied on age-old feelings of mankind, upon his knowledge of primitive cultures, and upon his own deeply felt intuitions.

The *Woman in a Chair*, 1924 (Fig. 51), poses in a deep tuxedo arm chair, reclining with left leg crossed over right, left arm bent at the elbow with upper and lower arms resting

51. *Woman in Chair*, c. 1924. Bronze, 13¾″ × 9⅜″ × 14¼″. The Hirshhorn Museum and Sculpture Garden, Smithsonian Institution.

on the chair's high arm, and right arm raised as though in salute. One may sense the relation of this work to the large *Floating Woman* (Fig. 67), through the gesture, the aspect of being lifted out of life into a spiritual plane.

The *Reclining Nude*, 1920–24 (Fig. 52), is something of a landmark in Lachaise' oeuvre, for it is the most extravagant statement to this point in the artist's work, though it was not cast in his lifetime. Measuring only 4¼ inches high, it is nonetheless an impressive essay on the female figure, reclining on a pallet, right leg thrown over left and drawn up at the bent knee, the right hip is raised in a manner similar to Matisse's *Reclining Nude*, I, 1907, while the upper torso is turned in contrapposto with shoulders against the pallet, right arm curved behind the back, and left arm stretched out against the pallet. This sensual pose of the full-breasted figure is a prophetic indication of the expressionist direction Lachaise' art would take in later years.

52. *Reclining Nude*, 1920–24. Bronze, 4½". Lachaise Foundation.

This work and other more domestic depictions of the reclining figure are related to the series called *The Mountain*. The first work to bear that title was executed in New York City in 1913, and was not shown for at least four years (Fig. 53). Subsequent versions were cut in fieldstone, 1921 (Fig. 54), cast in bronze, 1924 (Fig. 55), and finally worked up to nine feet for cement casting, 1934 (Fig. 56). The first *Mountain* was worked in clay, cast in plaster in 1913, and ultimately cast in bronze (Fig. 53). It embodies a concept of the reclining woman as an invulnerable absolute,[24] rising from the plain of human experience as a great truth of life. From tiny feet through slender calves to expanding thighs and enormous torso the mountain rises to its idealized head. In 1919 at the Penguin Club Lachaise showed a 17-inch version which E. E. Cummings commented on in *The Dial* as follows: ". . . it lay in collossal isolation, a new and sensual island. . . . Its completely integrated simplicity pro-

53. *The Mountain*, c. 1913. Bronze (cast 1930), 8″ × 17″ × 5″. Courtesy of the Oliver B. James Collection of American Art, University Art Collection, Arizona State University, Tempe.

claims *The Mountain* to be one of those superlative esthetic victories which are accidents of the complete intelligence, or the intelligence functioning at intuitional velocity. Its absolute sensual logic . . . perfectly transcends the merely exact arithmetic of the academies. . . ." [25] The figure rests on its right side, right arm and elbow supporting the upper torso, head thrown back as though listening, and legs extended to full length. The left arm rests on the figure's left side and the forearm folds back with the hand to left shoulder. The sculpture is, of course, a metaphor for the sleeping earth, symbolized by the fecundity of womankind.

In 1920 the fieldstone *Mountain* (Fig. 54) was shown at the Stephan Bourgeois Gallery. Cummings writes: "*The Mountain* actualizes the original conception of its creator; who, in contrast to the contemptible conventionally called 'sculptor,' thinks in stone . . . and to whom the distinction between say bronze and alabaster is a distinction not between materials but, on the contrary, between ideas. In *The Mountain* as it IS Lachaise becomes supremely himself. . . ." [26] It should be remembered that the great carved stone temples of India are intended to represent a mountain, or indeed a range. Not ordinary mountain(s) to be sure, but that *mountain* which religion and myth would say lies at the center of the universe. Lachaise extends his metaphor to simplify the forms, generalize the arms, amplify the torso by shaping it like rolling pastures, canyons, creeks, and bluffs. The figure appears to sleep—a new presentation of what is perhaps the oldest metaphor in man's memory.

In 1924 the artist took a plaster cast from the fieldstone version of the *Mountain*, worked directly on the plaster and then in the negative inside the new mold to achieve the handling appropriate to molten material, and finally cast it in bronze (Fig. 55). The shiny golden bronze finish which Lachaise selected for the work is in marked contrast to the mat finish of the fieldstone piece. Each material is recognized and respected for what is true and appropriate to it. Each new version gave the sculptor new insight into the meaning and truth of his concept. He held the idea, as he did for many of his unrealized themes, that the work might one day be cast in heroic scale.

Lachaise had been introduced to George L. K. Morris by A. E. Gallatin. Over the years of their acquaintance Lachaise did two well-known portraits of the wealthy young painter and aesthete. The two men shared a camaraderie of art professionalism that both enjoyed. It was finally in 1934

54. Opposite top: *The Mountain*, 1921. Black sandstone, 7⅝″ × 17½″ × 5½″. The Dial Collection, Worcester Art Museum, Massachusetts.

55. Opposite bottom: *The Mountain*, 1924. Bronze, 7¾″. The Alfred Stieglitz Collection, Metropolitan Museum of Art, New York.

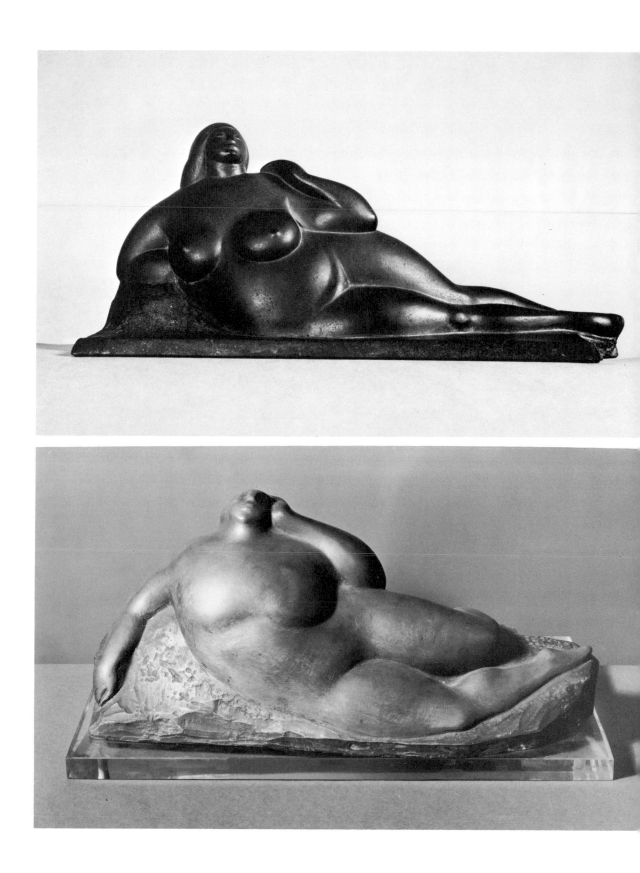

that Morris commissioned Lachaise to create a *Montagne Heroique* (Fig. 36) to be raised on six cement pillars on a rising hill in a grove of pines at his estate in Lenox, Mass. Lachaise planned to execute the work in about two months and hoped it would ". . . be great and solemn."[27] The piece took more than twice that time and was finished just before Christmas 1934. The massive figure weighed several tons and measured nine feet in length and four feet in height. It is one of Lachaise' largest works, embodying all of his reverence for woman in monumental form and heroic proportions. It is also the fulfillment of a theme that only he had worked in the twentieth century and one that bridges time for

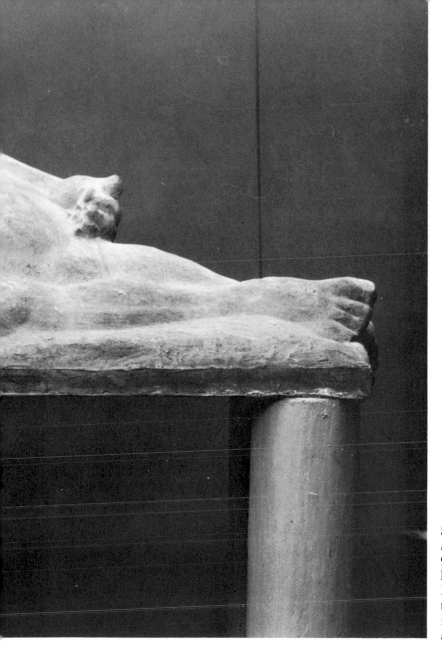

THE RECLINING
WOMAN

56. *The Mountain* (*La Montagne Heroique*), 1934. Cement, 9′ wide. Mr. and Mrs. George L. K. Morris Collection, Lenox, Mass. (Shown in installation at the Museum of Modern Art retrospective 1935, with the artist.)

its confirmation in Stone Age art. The figure's posture is essentially the same as in the 1913 plaster or in the elegant *Reclining Woman* of 1919 (Fig. 50). Though the arms are less tense, no longer folded under or utilized for support, the head takes on an almost religious formality. The sculpture and the idea had passed through a series of metamorphoses and had become ever more truly a mountain of unassailable grandeur. Lachaise and Morris had intended the work to become a part of the forest like the great Indian temples, and so it has become. The only showing the sculpture ever had was in the artist's retrospective of January–February 1935 at the Museum of Modern Art. Presently the work is grown over with lichen and ivy and could not be moved without doing damage to the forest, the sculpture and its patine of green. The figure's breasts, hips, belly, and thighs swell to heroic limits and yet it is in no sense overblown—a logical and inevitable mountainscape of womankind. As Kirstein wrote: "This sculpture is a clear phrasing of Lachaise' conception of weight, the balance of breathing sumptuousness, a mountain raised into air, earth sharing the shape of clouds, not swollen or inflated but placid, with a concentrated luxurious fullness." [28]

Bas Relief Bas relief sculpture is not numerically an important part of Lachaise' work. To be sure he did execute relief sculpture in plaster for the *Arc de Triomphe* on Fifth Avenue for the armistice celebration, and he did relief sculptures for Rockefeller Center (two separate commissions encompassing six panels), the Chicago World's Fair, the elevator doors in zodiac description, and for Wells Bosworth's home. All of these works were thematic, allegorical, or particularly associated with the contemporary need for architectural embellishment. They were workmanlike challenges, respectable projects which helped the artist to fulfill his financial obligations to his wife and adopted family. At the same time Lachaise did a number of mostly smaller bas relief sculptures over the years from 1915 to 1935 that were developed specifically out of his own aesthetic.

The *Dancing Nude*, c. 1915 (ex-Halpert collection), measures just 4½ inches and yet it is a rich depiction of the artist's muse, hand on hip, gesturing, in a dance step. In comparison with his statuettes of the same period the piece seems unsophisticated, archaic, even suggestive of primitive art. By the time he did *Standing Nude*, 1915–17 (Fig. 57), the artist's thinking had evolved to the point of depicting a nearly frontal figure with arms extended, evoking a power similar to fully three-dimensional sculptures of the period (e.g., *La Force Eternelle*, 12½ inches h.; Fig. 6). This bas relief has the animal force of the center figure in the Edvard Munch lithograph of *The Three Stages of Woman*. There is indeed a confrontation suggested by the assertive undraped figure which is accented all the more by the tiptoe stance, the challenging facial expression and the pose of the arms.

Reclining Woman, c. 1917 (Fig. 58), is a plaster measuring 10⅞ inches high in the horizontal relief. This piece sets a nude female figure reclining diagonally with

57. Opposite: *Standing Nude* (bas relief), 1915–17. Bronze, 7⅜″ × 4⁷⁄₁₆″ × ⅜″. Weyhe Collection, New York. Photo: Coe Younger.

58. *Reclining Woman,* c. 1917.
Plaster relief, 10⅞″, Lachaise
Foundation.

her head at the upper right and her feet at the lower left of
the plate. The left arm is seen in profile, supporting her upper figure, with facial profile and stylized hair treatment.
The right shoulder and upper arm are deliberately maneu-
vered into observable silhouette with the breasts and upper
torso depicted nearly frontally. In contrapposto, the lower
torso and legs are seen first in three-quarter view and then
in side view. There is a vaguely *art nouveau* feeling to the
pose, the treatment of the hair, and the depiction of the
legs.

   Dusk (Fig. 59), the 1917 floating figure in bas relief,
carries the *Reclining Woman* into a fully air-borne position.
The figure gives up its Munch-like challenge and its art
nouveau affectations for a sense of wonder and grandeur.
Lachaise has digested his influences to lift his muse into
a godlike, but ever feminine, posture. The lower torso is seen
three-quarter side view while the shoulder and upper torso
are turned nearly to full side view. Contrapposto is suggested by means that are graphic rather than sculptural in all
of the early reliefs.

   Nude Dancing, c. 1917 (Fig. 60), is in higher relief, with
the figure stepping with wide swinging step to the right, arms

extended with bent elbows to each side, head looking over the
right shoulder, with considerable torsion in the walking right,
looking left posture. This could well be an early essay on the
theme of the striding woman to be discussed in the late and
final works.

Nude on Steps, 1918 (Fig. 61), polychromed marble, is a
nude figure moving upward to the left with left foot raised
to the second step while the head looks to the right and the
right arm extends to the margin of the marble block. The
figure's head is cowled by a drape which is held by the left
hand at the base of the neck and by the right extended
hand, making a full backdrop for the upward stepping
figure. The relief is heavier than in earlier bronzes both
because of the larger vertical dimensions (nearly thirty
inches) and the artist's ease in working the material. This
slab of marble had three small vertical panels planned for
each side of its free-standing depth. The upper two panels on
each side have been removed and no cutting was accom-
plished on either of the lower panels. Two small bronze
panels, one of a standing nude with drape and the other of a
dancing nude figure, are known to exist and they may have
been prototypes for the missing marble reliefs.

59. *Dusk,* Bronze with nickel
plate additions, 5¼″ × 7⅛″ × ¼″.
Courtesy John B. Pierce, Jr.,
Boston, Massachusetts.

60. Overleaf: *Nude Dancing,* c.
1917. Gilded Bronze, 14½″.
Lachaise Foundation.

61. Overleaf: *Nude on Steps,*
1918. Marble polychromed,
29⅜″ × 20″ × 2½″. Lachaise
Foundation.

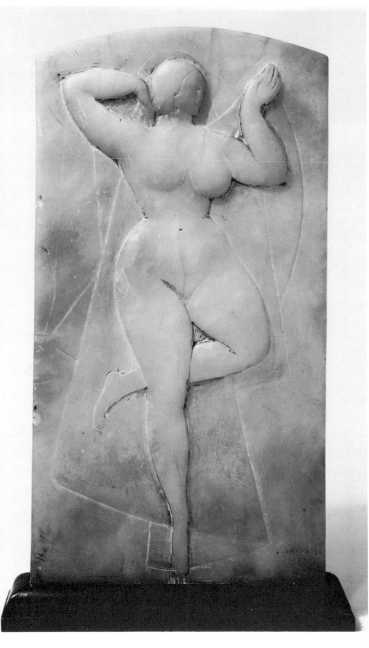

62. *Alabaster Relief*, 1927.
Alabaster, 13⅜″. Lachaise
Foundation.

63. Opposite: *Relief—Woman*,
1934. Plaster for Bronze, 87″ ×
30″. Lachaise Foundation.

Alabaster Relief of 1927 (Fig. 62) is specially suave and
elegant. It poses a nude female figure in nearly frontal position, weight resting on the right leg, left leg drawn up as if
in dance. Both arms are raised over the head, the right touching the back of the left-turned head, the left raised and
holding a barely depicted drape above the head which falls
behind the figure in a triple rhythm of folds following the
contour of the nude.

The large *Relief—Woman,* 1934 (Fig. 63), exhibited in the Museum of Modern Art retrospective, measures eighty-seven by thirty inches overall. It describes a nearly frontal female nude with right leg crossing before the left leg and standing on tip toes. The right hand is posed back-handed on hip and the left arm parallels the body while the hand is held in open-palmed gesture at hip level. Large shoulders, heavy breasts, well-defined musculature in the lower torso and legs in addition to the stylized backdrop of draperies complete the piece.

Lachaise' typical process of working out his idea in small, developing it through a number of studies, establishing a definitive posture, and then progressively amplifying the idea to an expressionist pitch has not been followed in his relief works. A number, like the 1915–17 *Standing Nude* (Fig. 57), *Dusk* (Fig. 59), and *Alabaster Relief* (Fig. 62), either relate to parallel developments in the three-dimensional work or to a separate idea which was taking place within the flying figure evolution. The bulk of Lachaise' relief sculptures tend to look backward to the Beaux-Arts, Lalique, and Manship or partake of the well-made but uninspired nature of that part of his work which was dominated by commercial concerns. There is an academic superficiality about some of the reliefs which suggests that the artist had not exploited his own working procedures in developing the most deeply felt expression of his ideas.

Acrobats and Floating Figures

The plaque called *Dusk* (Fig. 59), just over five by seven inches, is the earliest herald of a body of work that is of central importance to Gaston Lachaise' vision as an artist. This small plated-bronze relief, which Isabel Lachaise carried with her always in her later travels between New York, Lexington, and Maine, expressed a message of celebration. It is yet another homage to Isabel—a mythic presentation of her larger-than-life-ness and other-worldly levitation. Her full figure, with its austere visage, ascetic coiffure, extends itself in space, indeed a *Flying Figure* as it was indexed in the Gallatin monograph of 1924. The figure appears to move in space toward the left margin of the plate as though swimming in the relief space. The right arm is extended without effort and the left is raised as though movement had brought it closer to the shoulder. The torso is turned onto its right hip, presenting a clear view of the left breast and the rounded lower torso, with both legs silhouetted against the "sky-ground." The high placement on the plaque confirms the suggestion of flying. The lack of tension in the arm movements or in the torso and legs verifies the sense of gliding. There is no exertion suggested by the posture or the positioning of the limbs. Lachaise is expressing his own wonder and delight in Woman and her life-giving potency. He shows us that she may defy the laws which govern lesser beings—she glides in mature beauty.

The circus, the burlesque, six-day bike races, popular dance and jazz music were celebrated along with comic strips and other popular arts in Gilbert Seldes' *The Seven Lively Arts* in the twenties. From his childhood Lachaise was an admirer of circus performers, acrobats, dancers, and innovators in their respective arts. He was deeply touched by a female acrobatic rider as recorded in his autobiography at Yale University,[29] and he always responded to fresh experiences in the lively arts with untutored enthusiasm. Things *American*, from hooked rugs and weathervanes to the raucous jazz records of his stepson, from Hart Crane to the burlesque theater were warmly accepted as "flowers and fruits of a new species."[30] The *Equestrienne*, 1918 (Fig. 64), surely refers back to visits to the circus in his child-

64. *Equestrienne*, 1918. Bronze, 10⅝″ × 10″ × 4⅝″. Corcoran Gallery of Art; Gift of Francis Biddle.

hood; but it is very much a work of his early maturity, informed by the presence of Isabel and expanded to embrace an idea of proliferating female ovals which would become ever-stronger in his art with the passage of time. The female figure, seated sidesaddle to the left, with legs drawn up in modest posture, sets out an orchestration of emotion-laden forms from the head, the roll of the coiffure, the shoulders, breasts, and hips through the curve of the horse's neck and hind quarters. This sculpture measures only ten by ten by five inches and yet it is a physical celebration of animal vitality. Seen in small, the work was accepted as rhythmic, original, and noteworthy.[31] The prophecy of the work went unrecognized, for it had its roots in an expression that could awaken experiences of the life of all the races with reverberations reaching back to Willendorf (Fig. 8), Lausel (Fig. 10), and Ajanta.

Two Floating Nude Acrobats, 1922 (Fig. 65), appears to exist in various states. The Los Angeles County-Whitney Retrospective of 1963–64 exhibited the Vincent Price version. That piece is horizontal, juxtaposing the two figures with the lower figure "swimming" opposite to the upper (raised arm) figure. The two acrobats touch only where the upper figure's right leg grazes the lower acrobat's right buttock. The harmonies of the outstretched arms of the lower figure and extended legs of the upper one are closed, while the upward arching figure of the latter moves away from the counterpoint into negative space. The figures are conceived in Lachaise' mature forms and the movement suggested by the figures is measured and stately though perhaps incompletely solved. The second version of the sculpture is mounted vertically and while the two elements are identical the sense of their contrapuntal relationship is entirely different and less logical, though the individuality of each figure may be seen quite clearly. Photographs indicate that individual casts of each figure exist. This grouping of figures was a decorative experiment of original force and linear complexity, nonetheless it is contrived in its relationships, leans heavily on the sense of suspended movement and insufficiently on the full development of each pose. Where the *Mountain* (Fig. 54) is an *explored* problem and a completely original and fulfilled solution, the suggestion of movement here is incomplete and the work fails to achieve integration into a unitary statement. Like the undulating motion (suspended) in the *Dolphin Fountain* (Fig. 66) these figures illustrate Lachaise' concern with the concept of

65. Opposite: *Two Floating Nude Acrobats*, 1922. Bronze, 11″ × 2¾″ × 7½″. Mr. and Mrs. John S. Schulte Collection, New York.

66. *Dolphin Fountain*, 1924. Bronze, 39″. Collection, the Whitney Museum of American Art, New York.

motion. They are again an example of his will to conquer the tyranny of gravity which is seen in his floating women and the *Flock of Birds* in the Chester Dale collection.

The *Floating Figure*, 1924 (Fig. 67), exists in two versions: as the logical connection between *Dusk* (Fig. 59) and the *Floating Woman*, 1927 (Fig. 68). It is one of the earliest examples of a fragment figure in Lachaise' art. Concerned with the expression of supernatural powers in keeping with Indian Apsarases—celestial females of divine beauty— Lachaise lifted his muse into three-dimensional space. In the earliest version (not shown in this book) the artist abruptly severed the figure's feet from the ankle and the right arm from above the elbow. The left arm extends alongside the floating form of the legs in a graceful parallel to that joined motive. In the later version (Fig. 67) Lachaise removed the left arm at the shoulder, freeing the upper torso while dramatizing the sensation of levitation. The second state makes effective use of the three ovals of head and breasts and their counterbalance to the formal unit of hips and legs. One can easily be reminded of the manner in which the abstract symbol for Jupiter relates to the egg-like ovoid of Brancusi's *Leda*, 1920.[32] The *Floating Figure* is not an angel; however she *is* celestial, perhaps divine, despite her scale-defying enormousness. The believability of the sculpture is enhanced by the cutting away of limbs and the concentration on the two formal units, a metaphor of poetic idealism carried through experiment to unimaginable success.

The *Floating Figure*, 1927 (Fig. 68), was first shown in plaster at the Brummer Gallery exhibition in 1928 and was first seen in bronze in the Museum of Modern Art retrospective in 1935. Lincoln Kirstein wrote of Lachaise' concern for ". . . contemporary theories of space and time. . . . He had been considering the almost unimaginable curve of the earth's ocean horizon line, straight to the physical eye, but progressing into an infinite curve; over and above this, even more incredible, the convolutions of the earth's curves enclosed in other more enormous orbits of which our whole universe is possibly but a fragment. . . ." [33] No longer a partial figure, the ninety-six-inch *Floating Figure* is the fulfillment of this theme, rising in the air, balanced with an exuberance, lightness, and originality for which even the *Elevation* (Fig. 17) could not prepare one. The proliferation of rounded breast and buttock shapes creates a fantasy of sexually laden forms

67.   *Floating Figure,* 1924.
Bronze, 12¾″ × 17½″ × 6″. Fogg
Art Museum. Harvard University; Gift of Lincoln Kirstein.

which communicate in the most forceful manner, while trans-
figured in the myth-making process into an extra-worldly
spirit. The sculpture's arms are extended to either side, bal-
ancing, palms up, without the Greek articulation of upper
and lower arm, wrist and hand, but in a single flowing unit
typical of the suavity and fluidity of Indian sculpture. Lachaise has etherealized his earth mother, provided her with
the energies of all the gods and a sense of the eternal joined
in cosmic immenseness. As one sees the figure in the garden
of the Museum of Modern Art in New York, one has no sense
of weight or mass but only the qualities of serenity, strength,
and exalted womanhood.

A number of male and female acrobats exist in studies
from the 1920s. Gilbert Seldes wrote: "He finds the acrobat
transforming the familiar planes of the human frame and
bringing them into unusual relations to one another." Perhaps only *The Moment of Falling*, 1928, and the fallen figure
in the Fogg Art Museum Collection (1927) are of special
interest prior to two late female acrobat figures. The Fogg
piece is an atypical transitional piece which may well have
been inspired by a circus figure. It is as though Lachaise
found this experiment a way of seeing freshly and of

68. Opposite: *Floating Figure*,
1927. Bronze (cast 1935),
51¾″ × 96″. Collection, The Museum of Modern Art, New York;
given anonymously in memory of
the artist.

69. *Woman Bending Backward*,
1926. Alabaster, 5″ × 9″. Mrs.
Culver Orswell Collection, Fogg
Art Museum, Harvard
University.

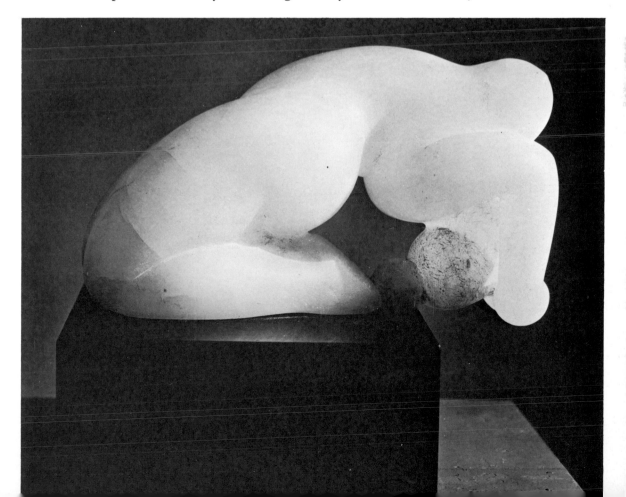

renewing his wonder in the richness and variety of possibilities inherent in the female form. *The Moment of Falling* suspends the figure atop a column, upside down with right leg and arm extended dramatically left and right, head down, implying an uncontrolled fall. It is an unusual informal pose which appears to confirm the circus figure inspiration and could even have been related to a performing tragedy. Lachaise has caught the full figures at their peak of physical prowess and beauty and introduced a desperate though regal gesture and the sobering recognition of mortality.

One year later Lachaise formed *Acrobat* (Fig. 71), pictured in the Museum of Modern Art catalog as Number 38.

70. Opposite: *"Acrobat" Upside Down Figure,* 1927, Bronze, Fogg Art Museum, Harvard University; bequest of Marian H. Phinney.

71. *Acrobat,* 1929. Nickeled Bronze, 20″. Whereabouts unknown.

72. *Acrobat Woman*, 1934.
Bronze, 19¾″. Whereabouts
unknown.

This figure, probably a circus performer, is posed in a one-armed handstand with her left arm extending from her shoulder as if for balance. The left leg is extended straight above shoulders and hips, while the right leg is bent at the knee with the foot touching the left leg below the knee. Worked in bronze with nickeled areas conforming to a performer's two-piece costume, the sculpture has a naturalism which suggests observation, at the same time that one recognizes evidence of amplification and rearrangement relating to the artist's expressive purposes. The figure's head arches backward to join the rounded forms of the buttocks in an imaginative play of convex forms. The fluidity of the legs and arms recalls Indian counterparts rather than Greek or Roman geometry. The undulant effect is sensuous, generalized, harmonious, and peculiarly timeless despite the pop art inspiration of the work.

Five years later Lachaise executed a second version called *Acrobat Woman* (Fig. 72), drawn out of the former piece. Like the later *Mountains* or the large *Floating Woman* (Fig. 68) when related to *Dusk* (Fig. 59), the work presents a new, more generalized, and fully rationalized integration of idea with the fugue-like arrangement of feminine ovals. The sculpture rises from the right arm in hand-stand, through the merging breast shapes into a baroque integration of shoulders, head, hips, and buttocks. It is an astonishing work, its only counterpart being the diminutive-enormous Venuses of prehistory, like the statuette from the caves of Les Rideaux at Lespugue. This work suggests even greater possibilities than the *Abstract Torso*, 1930, in the Whitney Museum collection. Lachaise' brilliant technical skills served his continually burgeoning vision of the female life force.

Fragments

Rainer Maria Rilke, the German poet (1875–1926), came to know the sculpture of Rodin in the early years of the century. With a commission to do a monograph on Rodin's art he came to France to meet and study with the older man. He spent several months in late 1902 and early 1903 with the artist in Paris and Meudon and published his first essay the latter year. Subsequently Rilke became Rodin's private secretary, and he continued to write and lecture until 1906 when there was a rupture in their friendship.

Writing on Rodin's fragmentary sculpture, Rilke said ". . . it is striking that the arms are lacking. . . . Rodin . . .

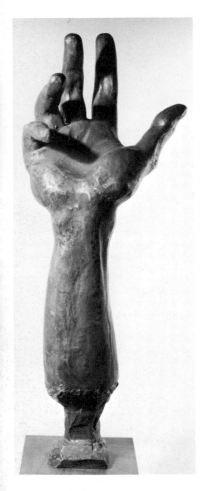

73. *Hand of Richard Buhlig,*
1928. Bronze, 20½″. Los
Angeles County Museum of Art.

74. Opposite: *Female Torso*
(*"Ogunquit Torso"*), 1925.
Nickeled Bronze (cast 1928).
Memorial Art Gallery, University
of Rochester, anonymous gift.

considered (them) . . . as something superfluous, something
immoderate that one can throw off—something unimportant
. . . rather like someone who has given away his cap in
order to drink out of the brook."

He continued: "The same completeness is conveyed on all
(the fragmentary sculptures). Nothing necessary is lacking.
One stands before them as before something whole. An
artistic whole need not necessarily coincide with the complete
thing. . . . new values, proportions and balance may originate
(within the sculpture). . . . It is left to the artist to make out
of many things one thing, and from the smallest part of a
thing an entirety." [34]

Prior to Rodin's time it would have been considered
perverse to present a fragment of a full human figure. It
violated the integrity of the body and seemed to lack the
correct idealism of sculpture. In effect Rodin gave permission to successive generations of artists to follow his experimental lead, which grew in part from study of damaged
antique sculpture.

In his later years Lachaise found an active interest in the
anatomical fragment. Perhaps his earliest essay in that direction is in the Orswell collection, being a figure from the
mid-thigh to the shoulder, with a drape falling from the left
hand held at the breast. The piece has a romantic air and an
undefined quality that suggests searching on the sculptor's
part.

It is known that Lachaise had the experience of drawing
from fragmented sculptures in the Louvre and from casts of
the antique at the Beaux-Arts. He was also familiar with
Rodin's researches into the armless-headless-torso, the *Walking Man,* and his reputation for cutting away an unconvinc-
ing limb or even of reconstituting a sculpture from a part. It
is also certain that Lachaise attended the Brancusi exhibition at Brummer's in 1926, saw Brancusi's essays in the fragment sculpture, and admired that artist's work.[35]

It is, of course, only a short step from the portrait bust to
the portrait mask—those hollow shells bordered by the hair-
line, the cheek beside the ear and including the chin, those
highly polished virtuoso descriptions of his sitters which
startle the viewer by their ability to summon up the whole
figure through the partial description of the head alone.
Perhaps these works and others like the Cleveland *Head of a
Woman,* 1922, emerging from the uncut stone, and the *Hand
of Buhlig,* 1928 (Fig. 73), were unconscious preparations
for later investigations of the fragment figure.

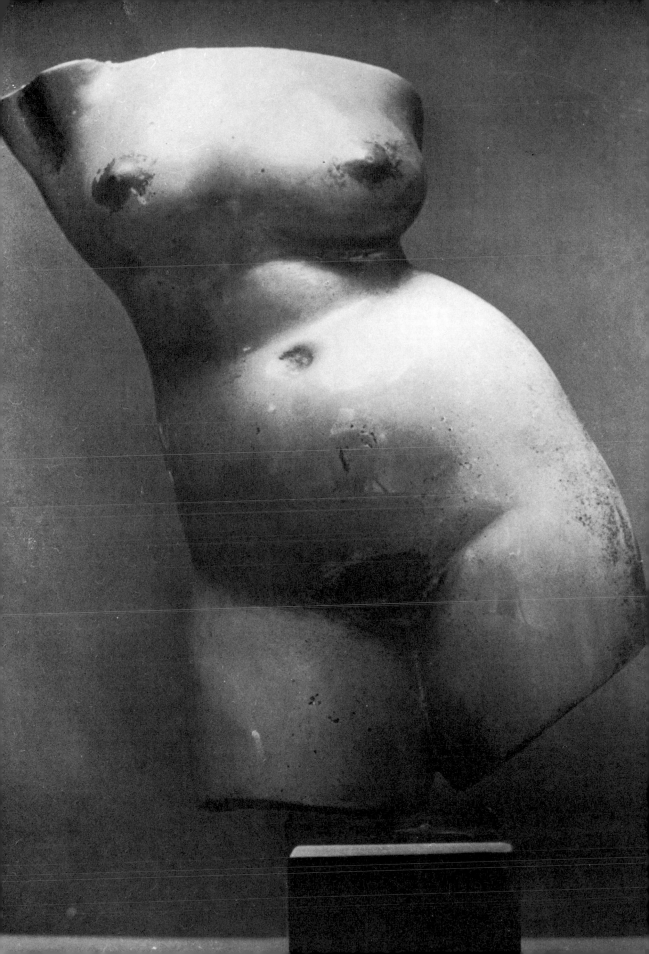

The so-called *Ogunquit* (Fig. 74) and *Classic Torsos* (Fig. 75), variously dated from 1926 to 1928, appear to be the earliest statements of the fragment without drapery in Lachaise' mature development. These bronze shells are not only devoid of head, arms, and legs from the upper thigh, but they offer only the front facade of the figure, incomplete in the round. These figures are nonetheless convincing, establishing a three dimensionality that belies the shell form reality and achieves an *all from part* sense of the figure and the muse which guided its creation. The *Ogunquit Torso* has a stretching *contrapposto* life with the left hip raised as though that leg carries the figure's weight and the right leg might be extended as though to take a step. The right upper torso moves upward as though reaching or gesturing and the right breast follows that motion while the left breast is lowered toward the rising and echoing form of the left hip. There is a rhythm of rising and falling, of openness and at the same time intimacy, as if the work had breathing life. Despite its shell-like formation, the sculpture has several faces and genuine three dimensionality. One senses the gesture of the right arm, the rising motion, and the consequent stretching effect on the right side of the sculpture relating to the compression absorbed by the left side of the piece. The weight of the breasts is dramatized by the contrapposto and made palpable by their relation to the hipline and the rounded movement of the lower torso's asymmetric volume. Lachaise' concentration on the implied movement of arms and legs, and the consequent reflection of that movement in the torso, has resulted in a focusing upon the essential that is so complete that it sums up the knowledge and the experience of *Elevation* (Fig. 17), in a 10½-inch bronze.

The *Seated Torso*, 1928 (Fig. 76), implies greater naturalism and less of the idealization carried in the *Ogunquit Torso*. Here the description is explicit, observed, less connected with earlier sculpture. The figure is truncated in the same manner at the shoulder and upper thigh, but in the later piece the musculature of the neck, the throat, and a touch of hair is apparent at the nape of the neck. The gesture of the shoulders suggests that the arms might have been thrown wide as if for an embrace. The torso is thus given a sense of being *uncovered*, of being bared in a gestural fashion. The upper torso leans forward slightly with the breasts falling with palpable weight, the pelvis tilts upward, with evident muscular effort in the abdomen so that tense musculature is revealed beneath the ample forms of flesh. The truncated legs are

75. Opposite: *Classic Torso,* 1928. Bronze, 10¾". Santa Barbara Museum of Art.

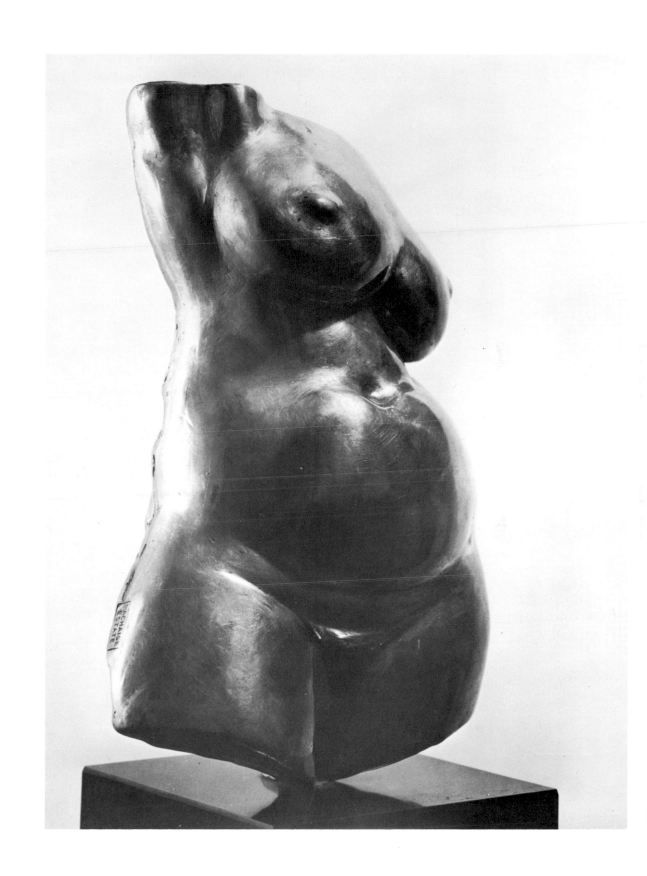

76. *Seated Torso*, 1928. Bronze,
9¼″. Mrs. Culver Orswell,
Courtesy Fogg Art Museum,
Harvard University.

widespread revealing the genital area with its prominent mons veneris. Not since the candid exposure of Rodin's cancan dancers (*Iris, Flying Figure*, 1889–90) had a major sculptor presented his muse with such a frank depiction of private parts. It should be clear that the work touches a level of expressionist strength, and a quality of sexual content that is rare in Western art. Lachaise has so concentrated upon the torso that the fragment is invested with intense personal feelings. He makes the sculpture more than real, even obsessively so. Casual observers may miss the emotional intensity of these works while others may be offended by them

77 (a&b). *Torso*, 1928. Bronze, 9½". Lachaise Foundation.

and turn away. There is a dramatic force about the explicit rendering of the piece that makes it pivotal in the development of the fragment sculptures, even when compared with the "Farouk" *Torso*, 1928 (Figs. 77a and b), and its mammary distortions. Having conveyed his feelings so forcefully already, there was apparently no way to increase communication through inflating the breasts.

The *Torso*, 1930 (Fig. 78), first cast in 1931 and belonging to the Whitney Museum of American Art, apparently was the first torso to be cast after the *Classic Torso* (Fig. 75). This piece has the same suavity, elegance of form, and closed unity as does the *Classic*. Measuring 13½ inches overall, the piece is again hollow-cast in shell form, depicting the buttocks, waist, lower back of the rib cage, and shoulder cap musculature. This tiny, apparently stylized sculpture has been referred to as an "abstraction" on occasion, in-

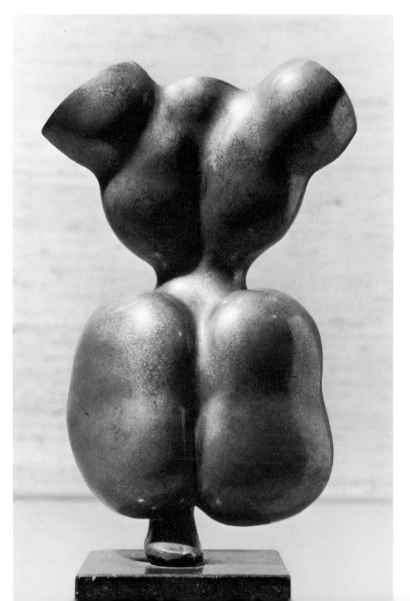

78. *Torso,* 1930. Bronze, 11½″. Collection of the Whitney Museum of American Art, New York.

79. *Kneeling Woman*, 1932–34.
Bronze, 19¾″, Lachaise
Foundation.

dicating that some viewers could not recognize the physical
elements which Lachaise was portraying. The sculpture is in
fact a literal rendering of the buttocks and lower back of the
Standing Woman, 1930–33, often called the *Heroic Woman*
(Fig. 22), and a more fully realized and finished version
of·the back of the *Kneeling Woman*, 1932–34 (Fig. 79).
Truly seen, the work is the most fragmentary of sculptures,
suggesting an upward reaching posture of the arms, an arching back, physical strength, movement, and life. The work expresses a mood of awakening or even joy in physical
well-being.

The *Torso*, 1932 (Fig. 80), which exists in at least one variant [36] appears more closely related to the same *Kneeling Woman* figure (Fig. 79) than does the Whitney *Torso*. Where the Orswell version apparently corresponds more closely in the treatment of the truncated leg flanges, the better known *Torso* of 1932 has been reworked symmetrically and the throat element removed. Sometimes the "completion" of a figure leaves it static while its fragmentation explodes it back into the movement of life. Deprived of its limbs, the sculpture has been brought to life. Just as the arms of the *Standing Woman*, 1912–27 (Fig. 17), become independent dancing elements, so do the breasts themselves in the highly polished golden brass finish. Again the sense of widespread arms and total openness gives the piece an expression which is generous, even expansive. While the viewer cannot but think of the gestures of the absent limbs, the tiny torso has an intimation of unity so that the breasts are not startling but natural, correct, somehow inevitable and in proper balance. The amplitude of these wing-like forms is made the more perfect by the neutrality of the treatment of the abdomen and the truncated legs. It would appear that the sculptor took more than one plaster cast from the emerging

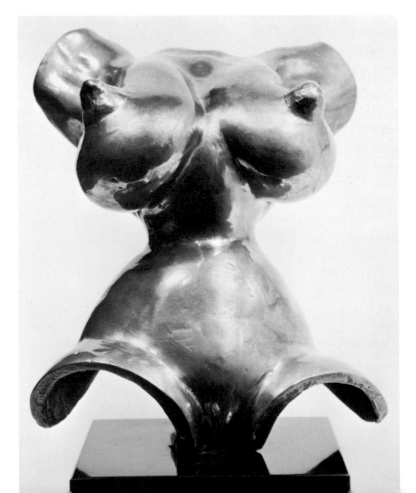

80. *Torso*, 1932. Bronze, 9⅝″.
Lachaise Foundation.

81. *Torso with Pendulous Breasts*, 1930–32. Plaster, 11⅜″. Lachaise Foundation.

kneeling figure and worked each to see the possibilities avail-able to him, much as did Rodin in various treatments of the arching bridge of the *Torso of Adele*. The finish on this piece can remind one of early standing figures, the *Walking Woman*, 1922 (Fig. 16), highly finished busts like the *Mask of Marie Pierce*, 1924 (Fig. 26), with its nickel plating, and the artist's concern for Brancusian reflections and light puddles.

The contrast between the positive, joyful, even radiant quality of this sculpture could not be made more complete than to compare it with another, the *Torso with Pendulous Breasts*, 1930–32 (Fig. 81), wherein the upper torso arches forward over the abdomen, legs widespread revealing the mons and vulva. In this piece, the breast forms drop for-ward with enlarged nipples, and the compression of sexual organs in the nine-inch fragment makes the intimation of birth spasms forceful. The dark patination is in opposition to the ebullient energy of the earlier sculpture. The *Torso with Pendulous Breasts* is surely an early work in the

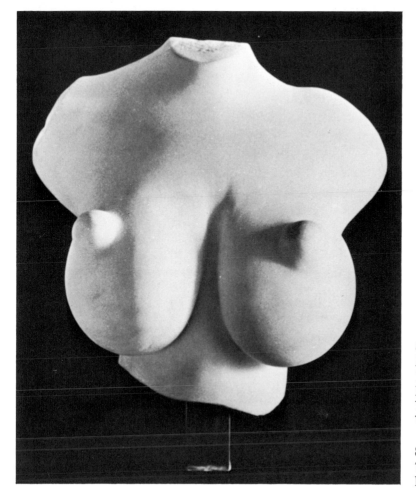

82 (a&b). Opposite: *Dynamo Mother,* 1933. Bronze, 10¼″ × 17½″ × 6⅞″. Collection, The Museum of Modern Art, New York; gift of Mr. Edward M. M. Warburg.

83. *Breasts,* 1933. Marble, 8″ × 7″. Collection of Mr. and Mrs. Edward M. M. Warburg.

development of the *Dynamo Mother* (Figs. 82a and b). (Also, see pp. 164–166.)

The torso titled *Breasts,* 1933 (Fig. 83), was carved for himself and only later sold to Edward Warburg when the artist needed cash. The piece is surely related to the *Torso,* 1932 (Fig. 80), with its bright and energetic qualities. The tiny marble has a generosity of scale that is surprising. The poet's metaphor for the loved one's youthful bust is given physical existence in this lightly-grained marble with its buoyant sense of vibrant life. The quality of exaltation felt in the *Torso,* 1932, is somehow spiritualized in the virginal white marble. The nipples fairly pulse with generative energy. One can only wonder how the full figure could have been solved had Lachaise the time to give shape to the lower torso and limbs that would complete this winged presence.

The marble *Torso,* 1933 (Figs. 84a and b), in the Smith College collection, is an unusual figure which emerges from

84 (a&b). *Torso*, 1933. Marble, 11¾″ × 12″ × 9″. Smith College Museum of Art.

a roughly cut block. One view shows sensuously carved buttocks with legs cut at the upper thigh. Another view of the piece has the breasts resting on the roughly claw-chiseled block. Arms are merely suggested at the shoulder joint and the neck cylinder is barely indicated.[37] What must have been an extremely difficult work in 1933 now seems beautifully and simply frank, the inevitable development of Lachaise' vision found in a particular block of marble. It is a certainty that the sculptor saw the stone with this sensuous fragment sleeping within it and cut away the excess. The modulation of planes in the carving of the buttocks makes the artist's touching knowledge of his muse and her immensely feminine form, flesh, and proportions quite tangible. The posture is (like the seated 1928 *Torso*, Fig. 76) untraditional, a forthright celebration of the unseen beauty in the human female. Lachaise has sculptured it in the virtuoso tradition, revealing the generous flesh and its support as the hips narrow at the waist and the planes swell effortlessly into the rib cage of the back. It cannot be presumed that Lachaise would have returned to this theme in later life for a more expansive development, even though that would have been typical of the artist's working procedure. The sculptural virtuosity of the piece's handling might well have reflected a concern for undertaking the theme in heroic size.

These fragment sculptures still have the power to startle with their obsessive and emotional investigations of female anatomy. While some of these works are experiments, most reveal themselves to study as fully evolved and completely realized works in themselves. The artist himself did not know how one work would lead to another or on later viewing seem to suggest an unthought-of avenue for consideration. The most certain of these works are absolutes in the same sense that a Brancusi *Bird* or *Fish* is an absolute. The fragment suggests the whole figure, its muscles and limbs and flesh, indeed the mind inhabiting it. At the same time each work is an exploration of formal relationships, often never studied before, in an endless flow of related parts. These parts function effortlessly in the completed work and are fully and thoughtfully articulated in a formal structure no less comprehensive and complete than a *Mlle. Pogany*.

The *Knees*, 1933 (Fig. 85), executed in white marble, is a work that might seem on first viewing to be a bland subject for so sensuous and passionate an artist. The seventeen-inch stone gives rise to two legs from mid-calf, which bend

85. *Knees*, 1933. Marble, 13¼″ × 9½″. Collection, The Museum of Modern Art, New York; Gift of Mr. and Mrs. Edward M. M. Warburg.

backwards at the knee and move into a sitting position, ending in mid-thigh. The modulation of planes, the growing circumference of the thigh as the artist works back from the knee is carefully calculated. The light play on the piece emphasizes these volumes handsomely. The work is "abstract" in a way that the buttocks (of Fig. 84b) can never be. At the same time both pieces enjoy the vitality and purity of new forms, freshly seen, and they do so with an unlikely grace and dignity. The *Knees* have a sensuous reality that is emotional in its impact. The tension of the flesh suggests muscle tone. The problem of the *Knees* is not unlike Brancusi's problem in *Bird in Flight*. There is nevertheless an erotic fantasy to the *Knees* that is belied by the neutrality of subject matter. Without renouncing the figure, Lachaise has expressed the will to abstraction of his generation while retaining the richly emotional associations of his personal life and vision. As a result, his art is even more heavily endowed than that of his contemporaries: Maillol, Despiau, Lehmbruck, Matisse, and the sculptors of an abstract vision.

Groups; Lovers

During his early years in America, prior to the time of his move to New York City, Lachaise began the first of pieces on a theme which was to become obsessive in his art. The theme of lovers lying together, side by side, was apparently first undertaken in Boston in a sculpture not over nine inches in length. The first study is known in but one unique cast in the estate of the sculptor's sister, Allys Lachaise. The pallet is not rectangular. The female figure rests on her right side, legs drawn up together with her left arm passing across her side and touching the lover's hand behind her back. The male figure lies on his back to the female's left, raising himself with his left arm to better observe his beloved. His right arm parallels her back and his hand cups hers. The work conveys her quiet trust, his watchful concern, their unity in each other. Roughly modeled, organized with certainty, the sculpture is a study for more ambitious expressions to come.

The Lovers, 1908–10 (Fig. 86), is a more sculpturally unified solution to the theme in that the female figure, still on her right side with legs pulled up, now rests her head on the male's chest and her thighs are nestled in the arch of his bent legs. This touching tiny bronze, a scant 4½ inches high, poses the man's left arm along the pallet in a protective gesture only short of an embrace. The right arm makes an echoing gesture while his head bends over her sleeping face to reassure himself of her well being. The sculpture's finish is somewhat more refined than in the earlier work, but the handling is in the Rodinesque turn-of-the-century manner. While the work is close to the earlier rendering of the theme, the intertwining of limbs better expresses the intimacy, reliance, and comfort taken by each in the other. Lachaise' protective concern is reflected very strongly in this work which is certainly a sculptor's tribute to wife and muse.

These depictions of lovers are undoubtedly reflective of Lachaise' passion and tenderness for his Isabel. At the same time he had certainly seen countless touseled figures in various stages of embrace in Auguste Rodin's studies for the *Gates of Hell*, the *Sirens*, and other ambitious works

86. *The Lovers*, c. 1908–10. Bronze, 4½″. Mrs. Oliver Wellington Collection.

visible to him during his student days and while working with Lalique. One such work, a variation on a relief from the *Gates of Hell*, is a smaller version of the embracing couple called *Vain Tenderness*, at the top of the left pilaster. "Probably conceived in the early 80s, it was considered in 1905 as the subject for a medal to be struck by Les Amis de la Medaille and to be titled *Art Embracing Matter*. It is possible that the relief was reduced to medal size in 1905, but cast . . . as *Protection* eleven years later (for the French Actors Fund)." [38] The work, reduced from 35½ inches in the Gates is just 3¾ by 1⁹⁄₁₆ inches in its silver medal existence. While the two figures may be standing in the gate, they appear to recline in the medal. The male figure appears to cradle the female who gathers her arms about herself and rests against his chest. His left arm touches her hip and the arrangement of limbs is less fully resolved than in the Lachaise versions. The *Gates of Hell* project was one of the most celebrated endeavors of Lachaise' era in Paris and could not have been overlooked by so avid a museum goer and so professionally informed a young sculptor. The posture of the legs in the medal could have been recalled at the time that Lachaise modeled the heroic version.

The Reclining Couple (*Dans La Nuit*), 1935 (Fig. 87), was a slowly evolved work for which Lachaise envisioned a great reception. It was developed at his studio in Maine and finished on his last day in his studio, summer 1935. He felt a compulsion to finish casting it in plaster and told Mme. Lachaise that it had to be done that day for a technical reason relating to his combining various materials which would separate if the casting were postponed. He finished the plaster cast of the seven foot pair with great effort and left his studio in Georgetown for the last time.

Lachaise called this large version of the Lovers *Dans La Nuit;* it was cast in bronze only after his death. In this sculpture the female figure again rests on her right side, with her head on the male's chest. Her left arm and hand rests on his figure and his right hand cups her left elbow. Their legs are intertwined in a more complex variation than the 1908–10 version. Her right leg passes underneath his and her left leg passes under his left leg and all of these limbs nestle attractively in a dazzling love knot. Again the protective static figure of the male cradles the pliable figure of the female in a complex interplay of limbs which conveys the artist's feelings of responsibility and protection. The

87. *The Reclining Couple* (*Dans La Nuit*), 1935. Bronze, 88½″ × 41″. Private collection, New York. Photo, Charles Uht.

faithfulness of this piece to "ideal proportions" would suggest that Lachaise held his expansive fantasy in check while expressing the anatomical verities he sought to explore. The piece would likely have served as a springboard for Lachaise to explore still more expansive and complex essays on the relation of man and woman had he been able to continue working. Surely many of the ideas he had worked in small, particularly the fragments (Figs. 73–85), the *Dynamo Mother* (Fig. 82), the *Burlesque* (Fig. 19), *Walking Woman* (Fig. 16), would have found their final form in more expressionistic, large-scaled works, in keeping with his major monuments: *Elevation* (Fig. 17), *Floating Woman* (Fig. 68), *Heroic Woman* (Fig. 22), *Montagne Heroique* (Fig. 56), and *Dans La Nuit* (Fig. 87). It is certain that Lachaise had a concern for the monumental and felt that it had been entirely too difficult for him to find the way to work on his own vision in the scale for which it had been conceived. It is instructive to realize that all of the large-scaled works excepting *La Montagne Heroique* were brought to completion (but not necessarily final bronze casting) without the help of any patron. His original and most deeply felt work, in terms of craft and his own passion as well as sculptural vision, were brought about independently save for George Morris' commission.

In 1920, in the second Bourgeois Gallery show, Lachaise exhibited sixteen sculptures among which were the bust of *Elevation* (Fig. 17), *Dusk* (Fig. 59), *La Force Eternelle* (Fig. 6), and *Love* (Fig. 88). The last-named work was a life-sized depiction of a male holding his mate in his arms. The sculpture was eulogized by Bourgeois in the foreword to the catalog and also received positive comment from Henry McBride. The idea of the male figure lifting the female into a higher plane was apparently part of Lachaise' thinking for many years (*Floating Figure*, 1924, Fig. 67; *Floating Woman*, 1927, Fig. 68; *Passion*, 1932–34, Fig. 89). The *Love* sculpture was shown in plaster and is said to have measured approximately eight feet in height. The work is to be compared with the handling and finish of the *Reclining Nude*, 1919 (Fig. 50), if one can judge by the frontispiece to the Bourgeois catalog. Unfortunately the piece cannot be seen inasmuch as Lachaise destroyed it shortly after it was shown in the January 31–February 21, 1920 exhibition. Conjecture says that Lachaise' normal procedure of working from the refined and academically correct treatment of a theme toward the emotionally experienced and amplified solution influenced him to destroy the work because it reminded him too greatly of his academic beginnings, and he knew that it was short of his real purposes for the group. Still another theory would have it that his financial efforts to bring the exhibition about had cost him dearly and that by the time the work had been returned to his studio he was behind in his rent and was forced to move; rather than move it to another studio he destroyed it.[39] At any rate the theme was important and it was not forgotten. The 25¾-inch bronze of *Passion* (Fig. 89), first cast in 1963, is profound evidence of the artist's devotion to the theme, and it cannot be doubted that he would have brought it to heroic fulfillment had he lived a normal lifespan.

In the *Love* group (Fig. 88) the female figure is raised above the male's shoulders, gesturing with upraised arm. The sense of two separate figures is related in the lifting, carrying service of the male to and for the female and is without the binding unity found in a Rodin *Kiss* or suggested by the intertwined limbs of *Dans La Nuit*. Surely the implications of the title and the nudity of the figures would suggest a state of dependence and of mutuality, but neither the time nor the artist's state of aesthetic development permitted him to find the solution to his symbolic depiction. Nevertheless Bourgeois, in the introduction, spoke of the artist's efforts:

. . . Adam and Eve of our times—imbued with the self-consciousness of a highly developed mentality, in quest of the lost paradise and the future.

The *Woman*, the moving impulse, in the involuntary stirring of a greater necessity, attracts the other principle, but fearing the subjugation of her personality, repulses him.

The *Man*, the directing and organizing impulse, hesitates between the attraction and the possible loss of his individuality, but cedes to the moving spirit—lifts her up, to be lifted up himself and with elastic body and soul advances blindly into the unknown.

Alternately taking and giving encouragement, struggling with the opposing will, both personalities refuse to fuse. But like the sea aroused by the storm, forms waves, which in continuous flux and reflux clash and lose their balance, attract and repulse, dissolve and reform themselves under the impulse of a greater power—so both principles of life are forced to annihilate their own will into the *Universal Will*.

With a gesture of her hand SHE indicates to his spirit the road to eternal beauty, which is created through her and for her. The Individuals are submerged, a greater world opens itself, where aspirations

88. *Love*, 1918–19. Plaster,
100″. Destroyed.

89. *Passion*, 1932–34. Bronze, 28″. Lachaise Foundation.

become realities, where matter and spirit meet, and where new ideas, new generations and new worlds arise.

The "literary" style of Bourgeois' prose has been commented on by both Cummings and Mme. Lachaise as overblown.[40] In the original 1918 show at the same gallery, Bourgeois had taken it upon himself to title works in a way similar to his "arty" writing. Nonetheless, Lachaise permitted these titles and this writing and may indeed have given Bourgeois at least partial direction in the development of his commentary. The theme of raising the woman to a height so that he might also lift himself to that height is verifiable in the art if not the words of Gaston Lachaise.

Passion (Fig. 89) is a more deeply felt and communicative work than *Love* could possibly have been. The scale and reticence of *Love* touched Bourgeois and McBride as pregnant with meaning. *Passion* transfigures the reticence on both a sculptural and emotional level. The female figure stands on her right leg, on tiptoe, reaching up with her whole energy to kiss the embracing male. Her left leg is raised, crossing the male's right leg and embracing it. The male figure stands erect, holding his beloved with his right hand at her knee and his left hand supporting her left buttock. They kiss, as they embrace, the embodiment of two beings submerged in each other. Truly a recreation of the *Love* theme but with a literal expression of the physical and intellectual magnetism the two spirits share. There is a communication of their ardent larger-than-life feelings that has its only counterpart in the seventh-century Hindu Elura at Khajuraho—the submersion of individuality in a union which is more than physical but reflects the very order of the cosmos. The sculptural unity of the piece is immeasurably more forceful than the *Love* piece as seen in lithographic reproduction. The expressionist surfaces of modeled, rasped, and planed plaster do not contradict the completely seen anatomy of the earlier work but amplify the meaning through more fully expressing the artist's understanding, passion, and sense of sculptural unity. Lachaise has paid his most ardent respect to his muse while developing a harmonious interaction of two figures melted together in mass, silhouette, and medium. In so doing the artist has achieved a timeless and meaningful work which transcends the merely cosmetic beauty and reticence of the large sculpture while expressing in tangible fashion one of the deepest themes in art or life.

Of the nine works selected for this closing section, only two were shown prior to the sculptor's death, both of which—the *Striding Woman*, 1928–31 (Fig. 90), and the *Reclining Woman*, 1928–31 (Fig. 91)—were seen in plaster in the Museum of Modern Art retrospective. The *Striding Woman* was subsequently cast in bronze and appeared in the M. Knoedler exhibition of January 1947. *Dynamo Mother* (Fig. 82) was first exhibited in the Margaret Brown Gallery exhibition, Boston, 1957, in bronze. Two of the nine works were first cast for the Los Angeles County Museum's retrospective exhibition of 1963–64, which traveled to the Whitney Museum, New York. The works cast for that showing were—*Breasts with Female Organ Between, Large*, 1930–32 (Fig. 92), and *Torso with Arms Raised*, 1935 (Fig. 93). *Kneeling Woman*, 1932–34 (Fig. 79), and *In Extremis*, 1934 (Fig. 94), were first cast immediately prior to the Lachaise Foundation's initiation of its traveling exhibition, San Francisco, 1967. The *Garden Figure, State 2*, 1935, and *Nude with Hat*, 1935 (Fig. 95), were first shown in 1973 at the Robert Schoelkopf Gallery, New York. It should be noted that the last-named sculptures and the *Torso with Arms Raised* were begun following the Museum of Modern Art's retrospective and were found in plaster molds subsequent to the artist's death.

Knowing the history of the exhibition and casting of the late works is helpful in following their selection. The two sculptures which were exhibited at the Museum of Modern Art were both reproduced in the catalog of that exhibition. Lachaise thus expressed double confidence in those pieces. Three or four of the remaining sculptures were referred to by Kirstein in the catalog as follows:

In his own studio at present there are a number of pieces in plaster and bronze which have not been included in this retrospective exhibition. Lachaise feels these works to be of paramount importance to himself and to the world's knowledge of him as an artist. If they were to be shown today, however, they might give offence and precipitate scandal obscuring the importance of the rest of his creation. He is proud of these works and he is not afraid of scandal, and he believes that the original elements in these sculptures will have a healthful effect when they are courageously displayed in a favorable setting. The elements characterizing these works are not new to him. But in them his previous tendencies have been pushed so far as to constitute almost a new revelation. He has fixed in these works heroic incarnations of flesh so violent, so disturbing, that for some time to come they can only provoke wonder.

With the two exceptions mentioned, this discussion is then

concerned with the works Lachaise did not feel able to show in 1935. They are works he held to be of paramount importance to his total oeuvre and he had confidence that they would eventually be seen creditably and with a healthful effect upon the viewer.

The *Striding Woman* (Fig. 90) and the *Reclining Woman* (Fig. 91), both of 1928–31, are blood sisters and ultimate recipients of the research, experiments, and discoveries of Lachaise' short but prodigiously productive life. One may see elements from the fragment sculptures (Figs. 73–85) and from the fullest statements of the Standing Woman (Figs. 1–22) and the Floating Figures (Figs. 59, 65, 67–70) in these energized, forceful, fully plastic mini-goddesses. The *Striding Woman* is, of course, the *Heroic Woman* (Fig. 22) moving out of her formidable and imperious stance into an equally impressive walk of life. Only seventeen inches tall, she has a vigor and vitality that is not exceeded even by her eighty-eight-inch sister. She has the same musculature, the same tight headdress, but she carries her weight on her left leg, which is draped, as she takes a great stride with her right leg. The right arm falls along the side, grasping the drape at the hip, while the strong left hand splays itself out boldly in the advancing right thigh. The now familiar torsion of the shoulders to the right as the legs move to the left serves to maximize the abundant energy within the figure and its undulant rhythms.

Reclining Woman, 1928–31 (Fig. 91), was one of only sixty works in all his oeuvre which Lachaise chose to show in his retrospective and one of only nine to be shown in plaster. Only 13½ inches high, it depicts a full nude figure, reclining on the right hip, with its weight cantilevered dramatically through the left leg's being swung over the right leg which stretches out parallel to the seat. The large-breasted torso and right arm in gesture provide a balance of opposition in this unusual sculptural equilibrium. The head is mask-like, composed, and the left arm is placed forcefully on hip, elbow akimbo. The hand-on-hip gesture is that of the *Heroic Woman,* as is the musculature of the lower torso. The vigorous and forthright pose and gaze serve to challenge the viewer. The *Reclining Woman* appears to stride, sit, gesture, and recline with equal vitality and unhesitating determination. It is a *pose,* an artificial posture, an unusual gesture, and yet the eloquent fullness of the figure permits an imperious sense of reality. More so than any other figure of the period, the *Reclining Woman* partakes of a popular

90. *Striding Woman*, 1928–31.
Bronze, 17½″ × 10⅛″ × 7½″.
B. Gerald Cantor, Beverly Hills.

91. *Reclining Woman*, 1928–
31. Plaster, 13½″. Destroyed.

vernacular ease, withdrawing from postures of iconic power
and with an acceptance of candid sexuality, even triumphant
energy, which is new in Lachaise' work. The sculpture is
self-conscious, posy, openly libidinous. The gesture of the
hand is not calculated to minimize this earthy sense of the
mother goddess.

The sculpture *Breasts with Female Organ Between, Large,*
1930–32 (Fig. 92), may never have been shown in public. It
was first cast in bronze in 1963 but was excluded from both
the Los Angeles and New York showings of the 1963–64
retrospective. It is an idealistic compression of breast forms,
erectile nipples and vulvar area into a 5 by 13 by 5-inch
bronze. It recalls the same combination produced in the
fragment *Torso with Pendulous Breasts,* also of 1930–32
(Fig. 81). (While it is not a full statement of a developed
theme it is the beginning of an idea that easily could have
captured the plastic fantasy of the sculptor.)

Late drawings and uncast sculptures found after Lachaise'
death reveal that he was pushing his work further than
the torsos, fragments, and acrobats discussed here. The

grandiose exuberance of his pencil drawings with enormous breasts show a proliferation of forms which go beyond anything the artist had done in earlier work. It was in 1933, that Edward M. M. Warburg, having purchased the *Torso* (now in Smith College's collection), the *Breasts*, 1933 (Fig. 83), and having commissioned his own portrait, then felt able to ask Lachaise about the direction his drawings and maquettes were taking. Lachaise admitted that there was a central work around which the new efforts revolved. He then showed Warburg the missing work, later called *Dynamo Mother* (Fig. 82), a name that may have come from Henry Adams' quotation about the animated life force and the source of generative life. Lachaise is reported by Warburg as having said that ". . . all of the new sculptures are related to the still unnamed piece in the spirit of theme and variations."

The *Dynamo Mother* measures only 10¼ by 17½ by 6⅞ inches overall. It is posed in a seated posture with legs widespread and raised in the air. The figure's arms parallel the gesture of the legs and the emotionally amplified breast forms establish a third pair of physical elements. The widespread legs reveal the vagina as if for birth and the counterpoint of legs, arms, and erectile nipples establishes an expression of the perpetuation of life which is unforgettable.

92. *Breasts with Female Organ Between, Large*, 1930–32. Bronze, 5½″ × 13¼″ × 5¼″. Lachaise Foundation.

Lachaise could not blush before sexuality. His life is un-
avoidably bound up with his vision of woman, birth, and
motherhood. There is no superficiality to this vision; it is a
personally explored series of variations that go back to the
artist's first years in the U.S. and to his lifelong love and
reverence for Isabel. Kramer went so far as to say: ". . . he
did produce one stunning work—the 'Dynamo Mother' of
1933—in which the abundant female figure is situated in a
posture of birth which is at the same time a posture of love,
with limbs radically foreshortened and sexual organs enlarged, and the entire sculptural mass modeled to convey
a surpassing sense of erotic vitality." [41]

Lachaise said at one point, ". . . there is a temptation to
repeat forms that grow out of contemplation of great works
of art of the past, like the Venus de Milo. This can make
for a repression of creative freedom. The obligation is to
create a new Venus with no loss of vigor." [42] This is indeed
what Lachaise was doing—creating a new Venus—a mountain, a standing idol goddess, a floating spirit woman, a
fragment of creative life. He was acting out what he had
indicated to his friends, that ". . . all art is a confession:
one can conceal nothing of one's weakness. . . ." [43] "You
have to go to a new bottom each time you do a piece of
work and raise it up, raise it up, otherwise you will go to
sleep, your work becomes only facility." [44] Lachaise indeed
dared to deal with "the organs and spasms of birth," the
problems of sexuality and even erotic content. They are indeed ". . . universal symbols for the source and continuation
of human life . . . (and) Lachaise has not been timid in
using these symbols." [45] No artist in all the history of the
world has dealt with these problems and issues so straight-
forwardly, so respectfully, or so truthfully. His knowledge,
technical skills, and profound intuitions have been married
to the love of one woman which helped him to express his
love, his reverence, and his sculptural expression of the
mysteries of life and the peculiar continuity and relevance
of sculptural art.

The *Kneeling Woman*, 1932–34 (Fig. 79), rests on her
left knee, with her right knee raised in a crouched position.
Her back is straight, arched at the waist with her arms
held over her head as though in prayer or supplication.
This is a figure closely related in its front to the *Torso* of
1932 (Fig. 80) and in the rear view to the *Torso* of
1930 (Fig. 78). The manipulation of plaster has been direct
and quick, the marks of the rasps and files are clearly left

on the surface of the bronze. The figure is very much in the continuity of the torsos mentioned and the striding and reclining figures of the years immediately prior to her creation.

The *Torso with Arms Raised,* 1935 (Fig. 93), was first shown to the public in the Los Angeles County Museum's retrospective of 1963. The sculpture is a fragment of a full figure, being the arms and bust of a female torso without a head. The arms are raised to shoulder height and the upper arms are held at near ninety degree angles with the hands posing with fingers separated in openhanded gesture. The missing neck and head has the unfinished treatment of a ruin. The large chest reflects a quality of aging, suggesting that the mountainous breasts have fallen, leaving the upper chest a worn reflection of the full-breasted youth of the past. The full arms, well-muscled but also showing signs of age, are indeed the arms of the *Heroic Woman* and of other

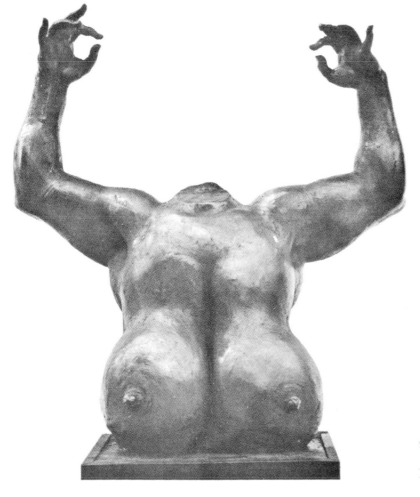

93. *Torso with Arms Raised,*
1935. Bronze, 37″. Lachaise
Foundation.

works discussed here. One can look at the figure, perhaps because of the absence of its head, as though one were a disinterested observer. With the head present one could not avoid feeling very much a voyeur. It is a gallant and affirmative statement of vitality and élan in the face of aging. It is nonetheless a commentary on the frailty of human flesh and bone and blood and, of course, the mortality even of goddesses.

In Extremis, c. 1934 (Fig. 94), is one of the most difficult sculptures in all of Lachaise' work. It is a small piece, measuring only fourteen inches in height and yet it bulks large in Lachaise' late work. It is related to the exuberant drawings of the late years in which gargantuan and pendulous breasts grow from ample, but by comparison moderately scaled chests. In some cases the drawings show women with two or more pairs of breasts, each of truly gigantic proportions. In other cases the drawn figure holds her breasts as in support or even hides her hands and arms under their bountiful forms. The title of the sculpture implies that the figure is dying. The head is thrown back from its shoulders with a suggestion of anguish or pain. The breast bone and rib cage is delineated in physical detail relating to the skeletons of dead animals seen in nature. Enormous breast forms fall to either side of the figure's chest structure at hip level. Huge nipples point tiredly toward the earth. The chest and abdomen are compacted and the vulvar area exposed between thighs and knees with the lower legs folded under the figure. It is an anguished work, reflecting changes in scale, amplifications and diminutions certainly deeply seen and felt by the artist. Surely Lachaise would have worked the piece through several variations before choosing to show it, rather than have it misunderstood or precipitating a confusing and wasteful scandal. The truth is that the artist made this disturbing and frightening sculpture in the spirit of his earlier proclamations of the energy, vitality, and life-giving capabilities of woman. He essayed here the problem of dealing with the death of the earth mother, the expiration of life from the bringer of food, the begetter of life, the transformer of blood into milk. It is a grim piece, a difficult one. It is nonetheless an important work of original sculpture, unique in the world, and a memorable experience.

94. Opposite: *In Extremis*, c. 1934. Bronze, 14″ high. Lachaise Foundation.

In his late and unfinished works, Lachaise was moved toward new insights, new revelations, unparalleled expressions of

95. *Nude with Hat*, 1935.
Bronze, 19″. Lachaise
Foundation.

the uncontrollable paroxysms of sexuality, birth, and death. It was not his method to find his way by a straight path. He always worked for that grace but he was nearly always denied its ease of discovery. He utilized his classical training, his romantic knowledge, and his full life experience to interpret his sketches and models, to study their communications in order to better express what was only dimly felt at first but which became ever more clear through refinement and clarification of formal elements.

In those principal works which he made for himself Lachaise continuously sought to express both subjects and subjective states of mind that were uncommon or unparalleled in prior art. He reached for passion, bereavement, tenderness, joy, the expression of sexual feeling, for the unknowable experiences of birth and even of death. His was a pantheistic expression of the artist's mission, not only having to do with art but with human life and experience, with mind and body, nature itself, perhaps only subconsciously recognized but converging in a single meaning beyond the intellect.

Epilogue

Isabel Dutaud Nagle Lachaise, the artist's widow, lived until 1957, twenty-two years after his death. Isabel Lachaise remained devoted to Lachaise' art and worked to support his reputation in every way she found compatible with her reverence for his art and her own very high standards. She urged the Whitney Museum to hold its Lachaise exhibition in 1937 and with Lincoln Kirstein's help another exhibition was presented at M. Knoedler, Inc. in New York in 1947. Exhibitions also were held at the Brooklyn Museum in 1938, the Weyhe Gallery in New York in 1956, and the Margaret Brown Gallery in Boston in 1957. Mme. Lachaise spent most of each year in Lexington, Massachusetts, to be with her son who was hospitalized nearby. Summers she spent at the house in Georgetown, Maine, and it continued to look as crisp and well-kept as ever. Twice each year she took two weeks in New York City, in order to verify her readings and keep up with the twin worlds of art and literature. Her son, Edward, died in 1963.

Isabel Lachaise' absolute conviction of the importance of her husband's work would not permit her to compromise it in any way. Dealers offered to take the entire studio workshop content for a given amount of money or an annuity but she was unwilling to renounce aesthetic control of the material, regardless of her financial circumstances. She insisted upon showing in only the most creditable surroundings, refused to sell plaster originals, would only work with foundrymen known to her husband. At her death the control of the artist's work passed through her estate to the Lachaise Foundation, under the Trusteeship of her great-nephew, John B. Pierce, Jr., of Boston. Under Pierce's watchful management casts have been made from existing plaster originals made by the artist. A limitation on the total number of bronze casts of any one sculpture has been set by the Foundation. Editions range from six to twelve bronze casts, the total number of each edition having been established to take account of bronze casts known to the Foundation to have been made prior to its organization. All casts made by the Foundation bear the stamp

LACHAISE
ESTATE

and are numbered consecutively according to the size of its limited Foundation edition. After all casts of the edition have been made, the molds are destroyed and the plaster retained or disposed of by the Foundation in a manner designed to safeguard against further casting either by destruction of the plaster or by sale or donation, with appropriate restrictions against further castings, to an established museum or other responsible institution. All Lachaise Estate bronzes have been cast at The Modern Art Foundry, 18–70 Forty-first Street, Long Island City, New York, under the supervision of Robert Spring, Proprietor, and Robert Schoelkopf, the New York art dealer.

With the cooperation of the Foundation a large retrospective exhibition was held at the Los Angeles County Museum of Art and the Whitney Museum of American Art in New York in 1963–64. In 1967 a smaller traveling exhibition was organized by the Foundation consisting of some forty sculptures and twenty drawings. This exhibition has been shown during the ensuing seven years in forty-eight important museums and university galleries in the United States and Canada. Coincident with the organization of the exhibition a publication including excerpts from many of the most important essays on Lachaise' art, photographs of the principal works, and an essay by Hilton Kramer was published by the Eakins Press. It is believed that through the medium of the traveling exhibition a representative group of works by Lachaise have actually been seen by more people from more different parts of the country than has perhaps been the case with the work of any other twentieth-century artist.

Notes

1. Edward P. Nagle. *Houdon and Lachaise*, manuscript in typescript, 30 pp. Beinecke Rare Book Library, Yale University, Lachaise Archive.
2. In conversation with the author, New Haven and Newtown, Connecticut, 1952 and 1953.
3. A handwritten holographic "autobiography" by Gaston Lachaise, 35 pp. Beinecke Rare Book Library, Yale University, Lachaise Archive. Probably written in 1931 to help Gilbert Seldes in the preparation of his *New Yorker* article "Hewer of Stone," April 4, 1931.
4. *Ibid.*
5. *Ibid.*
6. *Ibid.*
7. Kirstein, Lincoln. *Gaston Lachaise* (Retrospective exhibition), Museum of Modern Art, N. Y., 1935.
8. Lachaise, Allys. "In and out of the Dark," October 1964, manuscript. Beinecke Rare Book Library, Yale University, Lachaise Archive, p. xix.
9. *Op. cit.*, Kirstein.
10. *Ibid.*
11. *Op. cit.*, Lachaise autobiography, pp. 5–6.
12. *Ibid.*, p. 6.
13. *Ibid.*
14. Document in the Allys Lachaise Deposit, Beinecke Rare Book Library, Yale University.
15. *Op. cit.*, Lachaise autobiography, pp. 8–9.
16. In interviews with the author in New York, Lexington, Mass., and Georgetown, Maine, 1951–53.
17. Hartley, Marsden. "On Thinking of Lachaise," in *The Spangle of Existence*, typescript manuscript in the Library of the Museum of Modern Art, N.Y.
18. *Op. cit.*, Lachaise autobiography, p. 10.
19. Lachaise, Gaston. "A Comment on My Sculpture," *Creative Art* v. 3, no. 2, August 1928, p. xxiii.
20. *Op. cit.*, Nagle, *Houdon and Lachaise.*

I The Man and His Life

21. Conversation with Roy Gordon Carter, Foundryman, Art Dealer, 1953, New York City.

22. Gaston Lachaise Foundation, Boston.

23. Interview with the author, Lexington, Mass. December 1951.

24. *Op. cit.*, Lachaise autobiography, p. 11.

25. Lachaise Archive, Beinecke Rare Book Library, Yale University.

26. *Op. cit.*, Lachaise autobiography, p. 11.

27. *Ibid.*, p. 12.

28. Letter from Mrs. Alice Chapman to Allys Lachaise, September 4, 1950, in the Lachaise Archive, Beinecke Rare Book Library, Yale University.

29. *Op. cit.*, Kirstein.

30. *Op. cit.*, Chapman letter.

31. *Ibid.*

32. Letter from Gaston Lachaise to Pierre Christophe, May 1907, Beinecke Rare Book Library, Yale University.

33. *Op. cit.*, Lachaise autobiography, p. 13.

34. *Op. cit.*, Kirstein.

35. *Op. cit.*, Lachaise letter to Christophe, p. 2.

36. *Op. cit.*, Kirstein.

37. Lachaise letter to Christophe, November 2, 1907, Lachaise Archive, Beinecke Rare Book Library, Yale University.

38. *Op. cit.*, Lachaise autobiography, pp. 13–14.

39. *Ibid.*

40. Lachaise letter to Christophe, November 13, 1908, Beinecke Rare Book Library, Yale University.

41. Lachaise letter to Christophe, May 17, 1909, Beinecke Rare Book Library, Yale University.

42. *Ibid.*

43. *Op. cit.*, Lachaise autobiography, pp. 14–15.

44. Some writers have Americanized Dutaud, spelling it Duteau.

45. Isabel Lachaise in interview with author, December 1951.

46. Undated letters from Gaston Lachaise to Isabel in Lachaise Archive, Beinecke Rare Book Library, Yale University.

47. *Op. cit.*, Kirstein.

48. *Ibid.*

49. *Op. cit.*, Lachaise autobiography, pp. 15–16.

50. Undated letter Lachaise to Isabel, Beinecke Rare Book Library, Yale University.

51. Undated letter Lachaise to Isabel, Beinecke Rare Book Library, Yale University.

52. Undated letter Lachaise to Isabel, Beinecke Rare Book Library, Yale University.

53. *Ibid.*

54. Dos Passos, *The Best Times —An Informal Memoir* (New American Library, N.Y., 1966), pp. 23–24.

55. Undated letter from Lachaise, Beinecke Rare Book Library, Yale University.

56. Isabel Lachaise in conversation with the author, Lexington, Mass., 1951.

57. Letter from Lachaise to Isabel, Beinecke Rare Book Library, Yale University.

58. Poem by Isabel Lachaise, commented on by Gaston Lachaise in a letter to Isabel, Beinecke Rare Book Library, Yale University.
"Song"
My love
Is like a garden of roses
Great wide roses
And pale
That lie breathless

On the heart of night
Under the moon.

59. Lachaise' untitled response to Isabel's "Song," Beinecke Rare Book Library, Yale.
"Une belle godess au seins
    lourds au ventre
large et blanc et la pensee
    haute tranquille et forte
Une belle harmonie de sur
    la terre et vers
l'univers c'est un bel hymne
    que te chanter
Toi qui me donne La God-
    ess que je cherche a
exprimer dan toute mes
    choses
Je suis un Dieu par Toi et
    j'entours tous mes
instants de toi."
(Beautiful goddess
of heavy breasts and splen-
    did white belly
of sublime thoughts
of tranquility and strength
of harmony between earth
    and heaven
I sing my hymn to you,
You the goddess for whom
    I searched
Whom I express in my
    every work,
Have made me a God
You inspire my every mo-
    ment.)
60. Gaston Lachaise Foundation, Boston, Mass.
61. Mme. Lachaise in interview with the author, Georgetown, Maine, July 1952.
62. *Op. cit.*, Lachaise autobiography, section 2, pp. 1–9.
63. Interview with the author, New York, April 1953.
64. *Ibid.*
65. *Lachaise*, Brochure and catalog listing, The Brummer Gallery, N.Y., February 1928.
66. E. E. Cummings in a letter to his mother, July 4, 1918, recorded in *Selected Letters of E. E. Cummings*, Edited by F. W. Dupee and George Stade (Harcourt, Brace & World, Inc., N.Y., 1969), p. 48.
67. *Ibid.*
68. *Ibid.*, p. 56.
69. *Ibid.*, p. 63.
70. *Ibid.*, pp. 67–68.
71. Interview with the author, New York, April 1953.
72. *Ibid.*
73. M. R. Werner recalled this arch to have been built at Fifth Avenue and Twenty-third Street.
74. Memorandum from John B. Pierce, Jr. on the Lachaises in Georgetown, September 18, 1967. Daisy's "camp" was a one-room building, without running water in the woods on Robin Hood Cove.
75. Letters from Lachaise to Christophe, Beinecke Rare Book Library, Yale University.
76. *Ibid.*
77. Letters to Edward Nagle from Gaston Lachaise, Beinecke Rare Book Library, Yale University.
78. Hart Crane letter, 12.5.23, *The Letters of Hart Crane*, Brom Weber, ed. (University of California, Berkeley, 1965), p. 159.
79. Weber, Brom. *The Letters of Hart Crane* (University of California, 1965), p. 205.
80. *Op. cit.*, Hartley.
81. *Op. cit.*, Memorandum of John B. Pierce, Jr.
82. Interview with Mme. Lachaise at Georgetown, Maine, June 1952.
83. Hamilton Easter Field, *Brooklyn Eagle*, February 23, 1922, and Gaston Lachaise, "Letter to the Editor," *New York Times*, April 10, 1926.
84. Gallatin, A. E. *Gaston La-*

chaise (E. P. Dutton & Co., N.Y., 1924), pp. 11–12. The sculpture was never brought to fulfillment though Lachaise did complete the head and it was cast.

85. *Op. cit.,* Kirstein.
86. *Op. cit.,* Lachaise, "A Comment on My Sculpture," *Creative Art,* p. xxiv.
87. Cummings in interview with the author, New York, 1952.
88. Nakian in interview with the author, February 1952.
89. *Op. cit.,* Mme. Lachaise interview.
90. Hoffman, Allen & Ulrich. *The Little Magazine, A History and Bibliography* (Princeton, N.J., 1946), p. 197.
91. The last three to five pages of each issue of *The Dial* were devoted to a department called "Comment"— which constituted an editorial statement by the magazine's management. Scofield Thayer set a tone that is indicative of the owner's thinking, ". . . It has been *The Dial*'s habit to find intelligent reviewers and then to let them have as free a hand as any creative artist can have; no one has been instructed to praise or dispraise and delicate hints have generally had results the opposite of what we hope. . . . as long as we believe that the love of letters knows no frontiers we are going to praise them—we, including our reviewers. And the equal truth is that for a long time American writers have not been subjected to serious and severe criticism . . . and *The Dial* adds itself to the small number of journals which see no reason for praising a book except that the book deserves praise when viewed with the same unsentimental eye as looks out upon the literary scene abroad. . . . We fancy that not a few of the authors who have been mercilessly attacked in these pages prefer that attack to any suggestion that they are only in primary school and not to be marked on the same scale as the bigger boys abroad. . . . It is barely possible that our greatest service to American letters will turn out to be our refusal to praise or to publish silly and slovenly and nearly - good - enough work. The Americans we publish have at least the certainty that we publish them not because they are Americans, but because they are artists." *The Dial,* June 1923, pp. 639–40.

Beginning in 1921 *The Dial* editor announced a prize for the writer who best exemplified *The Dial*'s purposes which would be chosen from among those writers published during the preceding twelve-month period. The award had no relation to pay for the privilege of publication but was an award of excellence and a recognition of achievement. The eight award winners were: Sherwood Anderson (1921), T. S. Eliot (1922), Van Wyck Brooks (1923), Marianne Moore (1924), E. E. Cummings (1925), William Carlos Williams (1926), Ezra Pound (1927), and Kenneth Burke (1928).

92. Thayer, Scofield. "Comment," *The Dial*, January 1920.

93. Thayer, Scofield, "Comment," *The Dial*, March 1920.

94. *Op. cit.*, Hoffman, p. 199.

95. McBride, Henry. "Modern Forms," "The Winter of our Discontent," *The Dial*, June 1923.

96. Interview with Marianne Moore by the author, Brooklyn, N.Y., spring, 1952.

97. In fact there was no "commission" of the then usual one-third nature, but Stieglitz did reduce the income to the artist by from 10 per cent to 25 per cent for the "Artist's Fund" in order to help needy artists and perhaps also to keep the gallery open. See letter of May 27, 1928, Stieglitz to Lachaise.

98. *Lachaise*, exhibition catalog, February 27–March 24, 1928, The Brummer Gallery, 27 East 57th Street, N.Y.; "Here's to Lachaise" essay by Henry McBride, plus checklist.

99. *Ibid.*

100. E. E. Cummings, "Gaston Lachaise," in *Creative Art*, August 1928, pp. xxvi–xxvii. The article had been returned in February with a note suggesting that it was unintelligible to the editor of *Creative Art*.

101. Letter from Gaston Lachaise to Isabel.

102. Interview with Mr. Goodwin, by the author, N.Y.C., December 1952.

103. Gilbert Seldes, *The New Yorker*, April 4, 1931.

104. *Ibid.*

105. Undated letter to Isabel, 1932(?), Beinecke Rare Book Library, Yale University.

106. Interview with Warburg by the author, October 1952, Westport, Conn.

107. Interview with Morris by the author, Lenox, Mass., February 23, 1952.

108. Letter to Isabel, May 1, 1933, Beinecke Rare Book Library, Yale University.

109. Letter to Isabel, no month, 1933, Beinecke Rare Book Library, Yale University.

110. Letter to Isabel, undated, early 1933, Beinecke Rare Book Library, Yale University.

111. Letter to Edward Nagle, February 15 (1934). Lachaise mentions dropping out of the Rockefeller Center Municipal Exhibitions as were a number of other prospective exhibitors. Mme. Lachaise in conversation (1951) explained that the scandal surrounding the suppression of the Rivera mural bothered Lachaise exceedingly. He didn't admire Rivera's work but he thoroughly disapproved of its being painted over.

112. Letter to Isabel, undated, Beinecke Rare Book Library, Yale University.

113. *Art Digest*, February 1, 1935.

114. Interview with Allys Lachaise, New Haven, Conn., spring 1952.

115. Interview with Allys Lachaise, Newtown, Conn., summer 1952.

116. *Arts Digest*, February 1, 1935.

117. New Year's letter, 1926, Lachaise to Isabel, Yale University.

118. All of the following extracts are from the Lachaise Ar-

chive, Beinecke Rare Book Library, Yale University.

119. A. Conger Goodyear, President of Museum of Modern Art Trustees.

120. In an interview with the author, at the Museum of Modern Art, September 1951.

121. *Op. cit.*, Kirstein.

122. *Ibid.*

123. *New York Sun*, February 14, 1935.

124. *Brooklyn Eagle*, February 10, 1935.

125. *New York Times*, January 29, 1935.

126. *New York Post*, February 2, 1935.

127. *New Yorker*, February 9, 1935.

128. *New York Herald Tribune*, February 14, 1935.

129. *New York American*, undated.

130. *Art News*, February 1, 1935.

131. Interview with Mr. and Mrs. Fish, New York City, 1953.

132. Interview with Madame Lachaise by the author.

133. Interview with the author, March 9, 1952, New York City.

134. Henry McBride, the *New York Sun*, October 26, 1935.

II The Man and His Art

1. Ritchie, Andrew C. *Sculpture of the Twentieth Century*, Museum of Modern Art, N.Y., no date, p. 20.

2. Told in conversation by Mme. Isabel Lachaise with the author, Lexington, Mass., 1951.

3. Adams, Henry. "The Dynamo and the Virgin," in *The Education of Henry Adams* (Modern Library, N.Y., 1931), p. 384.

4. Isabel always claimed that the Stone Age Venuses were unknown to Lachaise. New and objective evidence would demonstrate the reverse. On the back of a letter from Lachaise to Isabel, undated, in the Beinecke Rare Book Library, Yale University, may be found Lachaise' penciled notation, " 'Art and "The Life",' George J. Cox, Doubleday." In pursuing that citation one finds the book published by Doubleday, Doran & Company, 1933. On examining the volume one finds Lachaise' name listed and starred twice in a roster at p. 115, and the 1912–27 *Standing Woman* reproduced from a drawing, which is apparently signed by Lachaise, at Plate LXX. Plate II at the front of the book sets out drawings of cult figures from the Eastern Mediterranean, plus the Venuses of Willendorf and Lespugue, among others.

5. Kirstein, Lincoln. *Gaston Lachaise* (Retrospective exhibition), Museum of Modern Art, N.Y., 1935.

6. *Ibid.*

7. Nougier, Louis Rene. "Prehistoric Art," in *Encyclopedia of World Art* (McGraw Hill, N.Y., 1966), Vol. XI, p. 582.

8. Conversations with the author, Stamford, Conn., 1951–53.

9. Conversations with the author, New York City., 1952.

10. *Op. cit.*, Kirstein.

11. *Ibid.*

12. Kramer, Hilton. *The Sculpture of Gaston Lachaise*

(Eakins Press, N.Y., 1967), p. 13.

13. Quote taken from the Diary of George L. K. Morris, December 21, 1931, and provided to the author in typed form, 1952.

14. Interview with the author, Brooklyn, N.Y., 1952.

15. *Ibid.*

16. Undated letter from Gaston Lachaise to Mme. Lachaise, Lachaise Archive, Yale University.

17. Interviews with Edward M. M. Warburg, Connecticut and New York, 1952.

18. Undated letter from Gaston Lachaise to Mme. Lachaise, Lachaise Archive, Yale University.

19. Said to G. L. K. Morris and recorded in his diary, December 14, 1931.

20. Lachaise, Gaston. "A Comment on my Sculpture," *Creative Art,* August 1928, p. xxiii.

21. Photograph obtained from Donald Goodall, University of Texas.

22. This is substantially the posture of the female figure in the two earliest versions of *The Lovers.*

23. Elsen, Albert E. *The Partial Figure in Modern Sculpture* (Baltimore Museum of Art, 1969), pp. 16–28.

24. See Erick Neumann, *The Great Mother,* Bollingen Series XLVII, Pantheon Books, N.Y., 1955, pp. 94–119. "With the Stone Age sculptures of the Great Mother as a goddess, the archetypal Feminine suddenly bursts upon the world of men in overwhelming wholeness and perfection. . . . these figures of the Great Goddess are the earliest cult works and works of art known to us. . . . Her very unwieldiness and bulk compel the Great Mother to take a sedentary attitude, in which she belongs like a hill or mountain to the earth of which she is a part and which she embodies. . . . The symbolism of the female godhead as hill and mountain persists to a late date in the East where the *hieros gamos* between heaven and earth is enacted on a mountaintop or on a tower symbolizing it, as in Babylon. . . ."

25. Cummings, E. E. "Gaston Lachaise," *The Dial,* February 1924, pp. 194–204.

26. *Ibid.* Scofield Thayer elected to represent this sculpture in *The Dial*'s portfolio of reproductions of contemporary European and American modern art—"Living Art"— with two photographs by Charles Sheeler, 1925.

27. Undated letter to Mme. Lachaise, Beinecke Rare Book Library, Yale University.

28. *Op. cit.,* Kirstein.

29. Lachaise holograph, Beinecke Rare Book Library, Yale University, Lachaise Archive. (See Part I, p. 4.)

30. *Op. cit.,* Lachaise, *Creative Art.*

31. Gallatin, A. E. *Gaston Lachaise* (E. P. Dutton & Co., N.Y., 1924), plate 12.

32. See plate 131, p. 77 in Geist, Sidney, *Brancusi* (Grossman, N.Y., 1968).

33. *Op. cit.,* Kirstein.

34. Rilke, Rainer Maria. *Rodin,* Collection, "Le Ballet Des Muses," Paris, undated, pp. 23–24.

35. *Op. cit.,* Kirstein. Confirmed in conversations with Reuben Nakian, Mme. Lachaise, 1951–52.

36. Fig. 80 is the best-known version. A variation exists in

the Orswell collection and is reproduced on p. 99 in *Arts Yearbook* 4, 1961, and is dated 1928 therein.

37. A bronze version of the buttocks segment exists at the Lachaise Foundation.

38. Spear, Athena. *Rodin Sculpture* (Cleveland Museum of Art, 1967), plate 82, pp. 63–64.

39. Kirstein, in interviews with the author, New York, 1952.

40. *Op. cit.*, Cummings, E. E.

The Dial. Also in conversation with Mme. Lachaise.

41. *Op. cit.*, Kramer.

42. Lachaise, Gaston. Preface to catalog, Bourgeois Galleries, Exhibition of American Sculptures, Jan. 11–Feb. 1, 1919.

43. *Ibid.*

44. Hess, Thomas B. "Gaston Lachaise, Revived a Decade Later," *Art News*, January 1967, p. 60.

45. *Op. cit.*, Kirstein.

Selected

Bibliography

Writing by Gaston Lachaise

"A Comment on my Sculpture," *Creative Art,* v. 3, no. 2, August 1928, xxiii–xxvi.

"Can a Photograph have the Significance of Art?" (statements by Lachaise and others), *Manuscripts,* no. 4, December 1922.

Preface to catalogue "Exhibition of American Sculptures," Bourgeois Galleries, January–February 1919.

Books, Articles, Catalogues, and Museum Bulletins

AMES, WINSLOW, "Gaston Lachaise, 1882–1935," *Parnassus,* v. 8, p. 5, April 1936, p. 41.

BOURGEOIS, STEPHAN, Preface, *Exhibition of Sculptures and Drawings* by Gaston Lachaise, gallery exhibition catalogue, N.Y., January 31 to February 21, 1920.

Bulletin of the Associates in Fine Arts at Yale University, "Sculpture since Rodin," XVII, no. 1, January 1949, no. 13.

CUMMINGS, E. E., "Gaston Lachaise," *The Dial,* v. 68, February 1920, pp. 194–204.

———,"Gaston Lachaise," *Creative Art,* v. 3, August 1928, xxiii–xxvi.

———, "On Lachaise," *Twice a Year,* 10th Anniversary Issue, 1948.

EGLINTON, LAURA, Exhibition Review, *Art News,* v. 33, February 9, 1935, pp. 3–4.

ELSEN, ALRERT E., *The Partial Figure in Modern Sculpture—from Rodin to 1969,* Baltimore Museum of Art, exhibition catalog, Dec. 2, 1969–Feb. 1, 1970.

GALLATIN, ALBERT EUGENE, *Gaston Lachaise,* 14 pp., 16 collotype reproductions (E. P. Dutton, N.Y., 1924).

GOODALL, DONALD B., "Gaston Lachaise 1882–1935," *The Massachusetts Review,* August 1960, pp. 674–684.

HARTLEY, MARSDEN, "Thinking of Gaston Lachaise," *Twice a Year,* no. III–IV, 1939–40.

HESS, THOMAS B., "Gaston Lachaise," *Art News,* v. 45, January 1947, pp. 20–21.

————, "Erotics and Eccentrics," *New York,* November 26, 1973.

KIRSTEIN, LINCOLN, *Gaston Lachaise, Retrospective Exhibition,* catalogue, Museum of Modern Art, 64 pp. 42 illustrations, January 30–March 7, 1935.

————, Essay, *Gaston Lachaise, 1882–1935,* Exhibition Catalog, M. Knoedler & Company, 20 pp. 8 illustrations, January 20–February 15, 1947.

KRAMER, HILTON, "Lachaise and others; The Orswell Collection," *Arts Yearbook,* 4, 1961, N.Y., pp. 87–100.

————, *On Art:* "Kitsch and the Real Thing," *The New Leader,* March 30, 1964, pp. 31–32.

————, "American Sculpture, Public and Private," *The New York Times,* February 13, 1966.

————, *The Sculpture of Gaston Lachaise* (The Eakins Press, N.Y. 1967). An anthology with abbreviated essays by Crane, Cummings, Hartley, Mayor, & McBride. 150 pp. 97 illustrations.

KUH, KATHERINE, "Lachaise, Sculptor of Maturity," Art Institute of Chicago, Museum *Bulletin,* v. XL, no. 3.

MAYOR, ALPHEUS HYATT, "Gaston Lachaise," *Hound and Horn,* July–September, 1932.

McBRIDE, HENRY, "A Sculptor of Elemental Rhythms," *New York American,* February 25, 1918.

————, "Modern Art," *The Dial,* March 1928, pp. 262–264.

————, "The Death of Gaston Lachaise—," *New York Sun,* October 26, 1935.

MELLOW, JAMES R., "Lachaise in Two Worlds," *The New Leader,* September 25, 1967, pp. 24–25.

————, "A Lyrical Celebration of the Female Nude," *The New York Times,* March 30, 1969.

NORDLAND, GERALD, *Gaston Lachaise, 1882–1935, Sculpture and Drawings,* Los Angeles County Museum of Art, 64 pp. 123 illustrations. Exhibition catalogue, December 3–January 19, 1963–64 (L.A.) and February 18–April 5, 1964 (Whitney Museum of American Art, N.Y.).

PACH, WALTER, "Les Tendances Modernes aux Etats Unis," *L'amour de l'Art,* v. 3, January 1922, p. 30.

RAYNOR, VIVIEN, *On Art:* "The Oldest Obsession," *The New Leader,* November 26, 1973, pp. 23–24.

SELDES, GILBERT, "Hewer of Stone," *New Yorker* (Profile), April 4, 1931, pp. 28–31.

SELDIS, HENRY J., "Lachaise—Study in Voluptuousness," *Los Angeles Times,* Calendar Magazine, December 8, 1963.

WONDERS, ANNE, "Gaston Lachaise," *Critique,* January–February, 1947.

WHITNEY MUSEUM OF AMERICAN ART, *Pioneers of Modern Art in America,* Exhibition Catalogue, 1946.